To _____

From _____

Date _____

Whiskers, Wit, and Wisdom

True Cat Tales and the Lessons They Teach

HOWARD BOOKS
A DIVISION OF SIMON & SCHUSTER
York   London   Toronto   Sydney

Niki Anderson

Author of What My Cat Has Taught Me About Life

Our purpose at Howard Books is to:
Increase faith in the hearts of growing Christians
Inspire holiness in the lives of believers
Instill hope in the hearts of struggling people everywhere
Because He's coming again!

HOWARD
BOOKS

Published by Howard Books, a division of Simon & Schuster, Inc.
1230 Avenue of the Americas, New York, NY 10020
www.howardpublishing.com

Whiskers, Wit, and Wisdom © 2009 by Niki Anderson

Library of Congress Cataloging-in-Publication Data
Anderson, Niki.
  Whiskers, wit, and wisdom : true cat tales and the lessons they teach / Niki Anderson.
    p. cm.
  Includes bibliographical references.
  1. Cats—Anecdotes. 2. Christian life. I. Title.
  SF445.5A528 2009
  636.8—dc22
2008044981

ISBN 978-1-4165-9068-2
ISBN 978-1-4391-0086-8 (ebook)
10 9 8 7 6 5 4 3 2

HOWARD and colophon are registered trademarks of Simon & Schuster, Inc.

Manufactured in the United States of America

For information regarding special discounts for bulk purchases, please contact Simon & Schuster Special Sales at 1-866-506-1949 or business@simonandschuster.com.

The Simon & Schuster Speakers Bureau can bring authors to your live event. For more information or to book an event contact the Simon & Schuster Speakers Bureau at 1-866-248-3049 or visit our website at www.simonspeakers.com.

Edited by Chrys Howard
Cover and interior design by Tennille Paden
Photography/illustrations by DAJ and Alamy

Scripture quotations marked NIV are taken from the *Holy Bible, New International Version* ®. Copyright © 1973, 1978, 1984 by International Bible Society. Used by permission of Zondervan. All rights reserved. Scripture quotations marked RSV are taken from the *Revised Standard Version of the Bible*, copyright © 1946, 1952, and 1971 by the Division of Christian Education of the National Council of the Churches of Christ in the USA. Used by permission. Scripture quotations marked KJV are taken from the *King James Version*.

To Zoe Marie Joyce
and all my succeeding
grandchildren,
And to
Christine Harder Tangvald,
my cherished friend
and career-long mentor

Acknowledgments

Bob, my incomparable husband

Janet Kobobel Grant, my agent and advocate

Chrys Howard, my kind editor

Ruth McHaney Danner and Leslie Burton,

my skilled critiquers

Margery Morgareidge, my "mother-in-Israel"

My prayerful and dependable friends

strangers, acquaintances, friends, and relatives

who shared their cat stories

The supportive team at Howard Books

CONTENTS

Introduction

TO the audience of adoring cat lovers
FROM Niki Anderson, a fellow feline fancier

If you're perusing this book, you are probably a past or present cat owner, or perhaps will be one in the future. My red tabby, Myles, and I welcome you—even if you've never owned a cat—to this new collection of cat stories.

Spanning the centuries is the affection of owners for their sometimes supercilious and sometimes doting cats. Like sugar in the pantry, cats prevail as a staple in families worldwide. Cats have surpassed dogs in popularity according to some surveys. These inimitable felines, around 90 million in America alone, strut down the hallways in one in four households. **They enhance our lives and inflame our love.**

Beyond the sensual joys cats provide, **their stories contain fables of truth that inspire growth in character**. Every narrative in this book unveils a spiritual concept implicit in the antics, habits, and endearing traits of this beloved pet. The forty-five pussycat parables in this assortment of tales offer the refreshing surprise that **God's wisdom abounds in both good and not-so-good experiences with a cat.**

This anthology includes a variety of cats in sundry predicaments and services—living up a tree; surviving 9-11; presiding at a veterinary clinic; brightening visitors at a lighthouse; facing death in a snowbank; patronizing a tea shop; comforting the cancer-stricken; bringing cheer at a prison; serving in a nursing home; leaving a memorial after Hurricane Katrina; plus other **amusing accounts of both calamity and compassion, each proclaiming a profound lesson.**

My compilation of feline philosophy is a pleasing mix; and while the stories portray the nature of cats, the messages reveal the heart of God. The underlying themes are commonly embraced by people of faith and also by many without a religious tradition.

A verse from the Bible leads the reader into the topic for the story. Such subjects as optimism, service, courage, companionship, and honor emerge from the behavior of the cat, the response of the owner, or the story line.

As you read, perhaps you will identify with Sam, the possessive cat, or with Flash, the fear-filled feline. Or you'll understand the reaction of Vivien, the resistant kitten. Or, like Lucky, you'll remember a foolish choice you once made. Maybe you owned a cat that brought you or yours the unique kind of comfort delivered by Lily, Calico, or Coco. Or having rescued one cat or more, you might prefer the story of Gus or Mom Cat.

And please don't skip these extras included with each vignette:

Purr-rayer: a ready response for the reader—something to pray

Kitty Wit: a humorous quip—something to prompt a smile

The Tail End: a snippet of feline trivia or a quotation—something to ponder

Finally, a brief description of the cat's owner—maybe, someone like you

If possible, I suggest you read the book with a cat in your lap. Between turning the pages, you'll want to stroke the elegant body of your God-given friend.

Whether or not you have the incomparable pleasure of owning a cat, may the stories I have recounted in *Whiskers, Wit, and Wisdom* introduce you to a warmly approachable, always forgiving, and wondrously practical God.

Other true cat stories by Niki Anderson:
What My Cat Has Taught Me About Life
Ins-purr-ational Stories for Cat Lovers

The Wonder of Winnie

Who among the gods is like you, O Lord?

Who is like you—majestic in holiness,

awesome in glory, working wonders?

—Exodus 15:11 NIV

PURR-rayer:

Dear God, when energy fails, enthusiasm shrinks and willpower weakens, may love persist to accomplish wonderful things. Amen.

Winnie the cat sat on a bedroom window sill breathing clean, outdoor air early on a March morning in 2007. At the same time, Winnie's owners, Eric and Cathy Keesling and their son, Michael, were inhaling lethal levels of gas fumes.

Floods from recent rainfall had filled the Keeslings' basement with thirty-thousand gallons of water. They borrowed a gas pump to remove the knee-deep water, but when the furnace cycled, gases leaked through a puncture in the pump's hose and circulated through the heating vents in the house.

1

Fortunately, Cathy had forgotten to shut the window where Winnie had been resting when the family retired. Eric, still mildly sedated from neck surgery that day, slept through most of the commotion that followed.

"About three o'clock," said Cathy, "Winnie began pulling at my hair with her claws, but I just couldn't fully wake up, and Winnie wouldn't stop meowing." The cat yowled louder and continued her pawing as Cathy drifted back to sleep.

Wakened a second time by Winnie's persistence, Cathy tried harder to rouse herself. "I kinda rolled over and as soon as I stood up, I felt like somebody took a ball bat and knocked me across the head, and I saw Winnie pacing in circles at my feet. Nauseated and dizzy, I fell back onto the bed, but here came Winnie, jumping onto the bed again. I think she was trying to tell me my boy was on the floor in the hallway," Cathy explained. "It was all too strange to be normal, so I staggered to the kitchen and struggled to dial 911."

In her stupor, Cathy had fallen during the phone call. Because the operator heard no report at Cathy's end, she summoned emergency responders—who rushed to the house. Meanwhile, Winnie woke Cathy again. Cathy returned to the bedroom, hoping to stir her husband, but "Eric wouldn't even budge," she said. Neither did Cathy yet realize that her son lay in the hallway.

When the deputy sheriff and a policeman knocked on the door, Cathy stood, dazed, in the entryway. "They kept asking me to open the door," she said. "I felt needlelike pricking all through my body and, I'm told, I was talking incoherently."

Just as Cathy collapsed, the officer opened the unlocked door. The deputy and officer lifted her out to the porch where she began mumbling concerns about Eric, Michael, and Winnie. They found Eric and dragged the six-foot, five-inch man outdoors. The morning chill shocked him to consciousness.

"When the policeman turned on the hall light to look for others, he tripped over Michael," Cathy said. "When they carried him out, I thought he was dead." But the officer had rubbed a fist over Michael's chest and revived him. "Though Michael used to think Winnie was a brat," Cathy said, "now he loves her to death."

> *Kitty Wit:*
> The most powerful of opposing forces
> are those exerted between a fleeing cat
> and the toddler pulling its tail.

The three Keeslings spent hours at the hospital undergoing detoxification from the gases. A vet examined Winnie and declared her healthy. The sheriff said if Winnie had waited five minutes longer, the family would have died. When the newspaper reported the story of the Keeslings' survival, the headline read: Winnie the Wonder Cat.

Years earlier Cathy had rescued Winnie when she found her as a lone kitten deserted in a barn. *Purr*-haps Winnie's life-saving acts toward the Keeslings were a thank-you gift. The six-pound, gray-striped cat with white paws and big green eyes is Cathy's baby.

The family had fed the two-day-old kitten with an eye dropper for two weeks while Harley, another of their cats, looked on. Eric sat up the first night to feed Winnie. Thereafter, the family, including Harley, kept a close watch on her. When she was two months old, Cathy asked Eric, "What are we gonna do with this little thing?"

"I guess we'll keep her," said Eric. "Harley's in love with her."

"Then we'll have to name her," Cathy said. They were fond of Winnie in the television series *The Wonder Years*, so Eric suggested they name her after the little girl.

On the night of the gas leak, the fireman who attempted to rescue Winnie must have been a frightening sight to the cat. In his bulky apparel and oxygen mask, he reached for Winnie in the closet. Cathy said, "I guess he looked like some alien." Hissing and biting, Winnie attacked him. Had the fireman not been wearing protective wear, Winnie, full of sass and spit, would have torn him up, he said.

Regardless, Cathy is grateful to Winnie. "I thank God every day. I know He works through animals. God knew if Winnie came to me, I'd know what to do."

The ASPCA selected Winnie as the 2007 Cat of the Year. She was awarded at a ceremony in New York. For the event Cathy made Winnie a superhero cape, trimmed with ruffles and appliquéd with a large white *W*.

Cathy said, "People say that cats knock over candles and start fires, but dogs save lives. But that's not true of Winnie!" The unfailing love of a cat saved three lives.

By adding extraordinary love to ordinary efforts, you, too, can achieve almost anything. You might even do wonders!

The Tail End:

Cats' senses are more developed than a human's. Their faculties of sight and hearing, and the ability to detect vibrations, are natural endowments, not supernatural gifts, as some believe. Cats also have a sense registering midway between taste and smell, through a receptor called the Jacobson organ, found in the roof of their mouths.

The Keeslings live in New Castle, Indiana, where Eric owns a hauling business. Cathy works at a nearby truck stop, and Michael, a student, is now relieved of fielding inquiries from the media for interviews with Winnie.

Home Sweet Treetops

And we know that in all things God works
for the good of those who love Him, who have
been called according to his purpose.

—Romans 8:28 NIV

PURR-rayer:

Dear God, help me survive the blasts of life with adaptability, faith, and courage.

For two years Big Boy was up a tree.

In 1998, when Hurricane Georges hit Gulfport, Mississippi, the silver tabby was blown off the rooftop of Gulfport Harbor Fuel & Bait shop. Big Boy and his sister had lived atop the roof during the months of their kittenhood, dependent upon their feral mother to bring them fish scraps.

When hurricane gales swept Big Boy into the limbs of the seventy-five-foot oak tree, he must have figured that one high place was as good as another. Relocated from rooftop to treetop, he made no effort to leave.

Hours before the storm, Big Boy's sister and the mother cat vanished. In the aftermath of the windstorm, someone spotted Big Boy. Repeated but futile attempts failed to remove the presumed orphan from the branches of the massive oak.

One of the Gulfport Harbor Fuel & Bait shop employees, Ron Roland, fed the oversize tabby for more than a year, making extra trips during wintertime when the shop was closed. Ron suspects the tough tomcat drank water from knotholes in the trunk. Cat watchers said Big Boy was never seen out of the tree—even when nighttime temperatures dropped to twenty degrees.

Kitty Wit:
After a cat forum, the round-table discussion on the subject of extinct animals led to a concluding comment by the feline facilitator: "A world without cats? I don't think so."

A lower north limb served as Big Boy's commode; ground-level evidence gave proof. On a south side, he ate proffered food from a tin container that Ron had nailed through the bark. But the feral feline kept his distance. "He'd let me pet him for a couple seconds and then back off," said Ron.

The cat's talonlike claws and head the size of a grapefruit put off a few would-be rescuers. Big Boy ventured from the timber tops only once. It was the day a bobtail trespasser sprayed on the base of the tree trunk. Roland, who sounded rightly proud, shared the outcome. "Big Boy came down and whipped him."

Word spread of the large cat in the odd habitat.

Tour buses began stopping so riders could view the strange sight. Passengers would ask the driver, "Isn't that treed cat somewhere in this area?" When the driver concurred, the curious sightseers pleaded for a stop. But tourists were sometimes disappointed. Given the gray striations of the bark and the gray markings of the striped cat, Big Boy camouflaged well.

For twenty-four months, no solicitation or enticement could coax Big Boy from the tree. A national wire service even released a feature article about the cat at the Gulfport Harbor.

But one day—unnoticed by all—Big Boy disappeared. Caring folks searched, but no clues led to the illusive cat. Had an owl carried him away? Maybe he encountered the bobtail again? Everyone had a theory.

Two months later an anonymous letter arrived at the newspaper office disclosing his capture. Big Boy had been given a "better life," wrote the sender.

Since the catnapped fellow isn't available for comment, we'll never know if he regards his new life as better. His many well-wishers hope so.

One thing is clear. While he lived in the oak, Big Boy made the best of his branches.

In the end the moxie cat gained a ground-level home with an owner who was—as most people believe—a compassionate rescuer.

Though storms bring unwelcome destruction, the challenges brought by change are often yoked with touching outcomes and pleasing resolutions. Howling winds are frequently mixed with a rainfall of blessing.

 The Tail End:

...an still believe that a day comes for us
..., however far off it may be, when we shall
...derstand, [when] these tragedies that now
...cken and darken the very air of heaven
... us, will sink into places in a scheme so
...gust, so magnificent, so joyful, that we
...all laugh for wonder and delight.

—Arthur Christopher Bacon

...llowing Hurricane Katrina, Niki lost
...ntact with Big Boy's friend, Ron Roland,
... Mississippi fisherman. Her thoughts
...clude Mr. Roland and his family and other
...rricane victims.

Only Out of View

Blessed are those who

have not seen and yet have believed.

—John 20:29 NIV

PURR-rayer:

Dear God, help me rest securely when you are out of human view.

Though Myles is bashful, he can also be a sermon on four furry feet.

When friends or relatives arrive, my marmalade cat usually retreats under the bed. If newcomers visit, Myles's rare and covert appearances are fleeting at best. With furtive glances left and right, he slinks to his food bowl for a nibble, and then quickly withdraws to a hideout. I call Myles "my shy guy." But God used this timid cat to refresh my faith in the fact of God's constant presence.

That particular day Myles and I were home alone. He lay beside me with his head propped against the arm of the wingback chair in his usual Mom-and-me position.

Our daily practice of quiet time nurtures us. I read my Bible, write in my journal, or lean my head against the plaid headrest for moments of prayer. Intermittently, I sweep my hand along Myles's soft spine.

That morning the doorbell rang before eight o'clock, also before my first cup of coffee and my cosmetic makeover. My fair complexion and pale lips matched my dove-white nightgown. "Oh-h-h, dear," I mumbled. A bulky bathrobe and boot-style slippers still adorned my stiff morning body. *Must I answer the door?* Myles raised his head with equal apprehension.

Whew, I thought to myself after peeking out the window. The caller was only the neighbor girl. She had seen my earthy look many times before when I was sweaty in the garden or dusty with flour while baking. I greeted Julia and learned that she needed a small bandage. I fulfilled her request and scuffed back to my chair.

But where was Myles? No orange curvature awaited me in the seat of the wingback. I called, but he failed to saunter into view as usual. Had he darted past me at the doorway and skittered out for a morning run? An expert at exits, he had fooled me before with his swift and sneaky escapes.

I began a thorough indoor search to his frequent places of hiding. Under three beds, I craned my neck looking for Myles. I checked the velvet parlor chair, but no Myles curled in repose. I checked his basket and the satin cushion on the dining chair, and in the basement, the place he liked the least.

Frantic, I quickly dressed while planning to conduct an outdoor hunt. Just before I stepped onto the porch, I took a final glance toward my chair. I sighed with relief to see Myles crawling out from the underside of the wingback chair. He moseyed toward me as if to say, *Sheesh! I was right here all the time under our chair, as close as I could get to you and still be out of sight from that intruder.*

Why didn't I think to look there? I puzzled.

He hadn't been far away. In fact, though unseen, he was waiting for me near the place where I had left him. Yet I was thinking the worst. *He's slipped out. He's lost. He may never return.*

I snatched him up, held him close, and kissed his whiskered cheek, then placed him back in the chair.

> ### Kitty Wit:
> The *New York Times* described Morris the cat as "the Robert Redford of Catdom." His "*rats*-to-riches" story includes the fact that before he was famous, the truck for the Hinsdale Humane Society picked him up for keeping several families awake at night while he romanced his lady friends.

Though my quiet hour had been interrupted, I discerned a heaven-sent message in the incident. My fretfulness over Myles mimicked the anxiety I feel when God seems to disappear. If the circumstances of life fail to verify God's presence, I panic. Why do I insist on empirical proof of His guardianship? The promise of God's dependability should be enough to anchor my trust.

God is never absent but at times He remains out of sight. When my world is troubled, will I remember to trust him if He is unseen? Will I be confident He is close by and waiting for the right time to reveal Himself? Will I doubt His watchfulness and look for a sign, or will I believe in His love and know He is near?

The Tail End:

The nose knows! A cat's sense of smell serves a major part in a cat's life even from the day of its birth. When you move to a new location, show your cat a piece of furniture from the previous home. The familiar scent will help the pet adjust more quickly.

Myles is the only sibling remaining of the three red tabbies whose stories are told in Niki Anderson's two previous collections of true cat stories. Now twelve years old, this handsome feline is pictured with the author on the jacket flap and the back cover of her books.

Good Mews!

Even when I am old and gray,

do not forsake me, O God, till I declare

your power to the next generation.

—Psalm 71:18 NIV

PURR-rayer:

Dear God, in my elder years help me offer the public at least one talent I can still use well.

An aging black cat with a predilection for the newspaper made front-page news in the *Spokesman-Review*. Guy Smith and Chris Eder's adopted house cat was featured as the newspaper's honorary feline in the year 2000. Many would agree that the cat's service to elders and children during his senior years exceeded the honor of his newsworthy award.

The Spokane, Washington, daily paper had solicited nominations for the purr-stigious appointment for Feline of the Year. The big cat's affinity for journalism helped him win the title. The cat's name, Paperweight, and his love of newsprint played largely in the judges' decision.

The article announcing Paperweight as the winner carried a headline with the word "pudgy" to describe the cat. Journalist and contest host Paul Turner wondered if the eighteen-pound tomcat would be touchy about the adjective. An e-mail response, signed

"Paperweight," helped dismiss Turner's concern. It read, "Neither I nor my humans are offended."

Paperweight loves to lie on the newspaper. He prefers the Sunday edition. The weekend inserts, extra flyers, and advertisements provide an array of paper and the heady scent of ink. Chris said, "I usually spread the paper across the floor and stretch out with a section at a time." Paperweight treads across the scatter of articles, essays, and photos, denting the pages and reveling in the noise of rattling paper. Chris supposes it's Paperweight's way of staying on top of current affairs.

Guy, a student at Washington State University, and his wife, Chris, had two dogs long before Paperweight joined the household. "We didn't intend on adding another animal to our small home," said Chris. But the meandering cat kept showing up in the yard. He darted from one bush to another, watchful, "but never in your face," Chris remarked. "Then he was gone."

Until one day. "My work colleague collapsed on the job," said Chris, "and I had to rush her to the hospital. Later at home, I stepped outdoors with my cell phone while tearfully relating the scary event to my mom. The cat approached and began weaving around and between my legs with alternating head rubs as I was sobbing." And he stayed.

Guy and Chris suspected Paperweight was displaced, so they began feeding him. Neither of them had experience with cats. Thus, Paperweight's first meal was a mere quarter of a can of food. Later remembering the small portion, they speculated that Paperweight was likely wondering, *What's with the meager serving?*

The first few nights they locked their boarder in the bathroom but he wailed his complaint and shredded the shower curtain. Despite the damage, Chris and Guy proceeded responsibly.

Next on the agenda was a scheduled exam with a DVM (veterinarian). "We had contacted neighbors and called the pound and shelters to see if the cat was reported missing. We learned from the police that if you harbor an unclaimed animal for ten days, the pet is yours to keep. We figured we'd done all we could," said Chris.

> *Kitty Wit:*
> Long before self-cleaning ovens,
> there were self-cleaning cats.

The vet suggested the oversize panther lookalike deserved a name that hinted at his size. But naming the heavyweight was a hefty job. They couldn't decide on a suitable moniker for the corpulent cat. Tank? Brutus? Goliath?

One morning dawned with more than sunrise. "Guy awoke with the cat propped against his leg," said Chris. "Guy groaned, rolled over, and grumbled, 'Get that paperweight off my leg!'"

"Paperweight!" Chris exclaimed. "We'll name him Paperweight!"

Obviously, a paperweight must be heavy enough to hold things down. On that point, Paperweight was qualified. While sharing the household with a Labrador and a beagle, he had secured his position. Moreover, he was immovable when he settled himself in either of the dogs' beds.

One hurdle of adjustment remained—making him an indoor-only resident. After five minor surgeries for injuries incurred during jaunts in the neighborhood, Paperweight was an obvious risk as an outdoor cat. Once he resigned himself to indoor life, he accepted his confinement with good behavior. He chose the scratching post over furniture and always used the litter box. He respected the houseplants, not even nibbling the catmint.

Among Paperweight's virtues as the *Spokesman-Review*'s honorary feline was his devotion to the young and elderly through People-Pet Partnership. After passing a temperament test, he collaborated with PPP by visiting residents at longterm-care facilities. Accompanied by Chris or Guy, he went to a nursing home every Sunday for two years. He lay on pillows, shoulders, and laps, purring his pleasure and offering comfort. "He was particularly fond of one octogenarian who loved to stroke him," said Chris.

People-Pet Partnership also sponsored trips to elementary schools to teach children the proper care of pets. The unflappable Paperweight remained calm even when students squealed with delight or reached to pet him.

Though he had aged, Paperweight refused to retire. The senior kitty-zen had found new purpose in his declining years through his services at nursing homes and schools.

Like Paperweight, in the last decades of life you may finally have time for the newspaper. Between reading daily editions, make some news of your own. Strengthen society with a contribution of service.

 The Tail End:

You don't need nine lives to make a difference in the world.

Chris and Guy live in the Pacific Northwest. Guy teaches at a community college and Chris works in higher education. They enjoy their beagle, Basil, and walking on beaches and through parks nearby. The couple also raises puppies for Guide Dogs for the Blind, Inc. Paperweight was their first and only cat and is greatly missed.

Mercy Me!

Do not withhold your mercy from me,

O Lord, may your love

and your truth always protect me.

—Psalm 40:11 NIV

PURR-rayer:

Dear God, I thank you for traveling mercies.

There were safer ways to hitch a ride but don't suggest them to a six-week-old kitten named Lucky. Thankfully, when youthful ignorance leads to risky choices, the youthful are often spared.

The kitten's family, the Pendells, shared their life with two adult cats and the litter of one queen. In a shed near the driveway, the outdoor cats were fed and sheltered. With eight furry critters traversing the property and parking area, the Pendells were vigilant about surveying the driveway before pulling in or backing out.

Becki, their twenty-two-year-old daughter, set out on a two-hundred-mile trip from Benton City, Washington, to Seattle. As her custom, she first pounded on the car hood so nearby cats would scatter. Then she turned the key and inched the car forward to make sure none lay resting in the shade under her Honda. Convinced the way was clear, she backed out and began thinking ahead to her friends' wedding in the big city seaport of western Washington. She was a bridesmaid.

Rested by the soft hum of the engine and the majestic display of the Cascade Mountains, Becki drove westward. She gave herself a brief reprieve from the steering wheel with two quick stops. In North Bend, Becki took a lunch break, and in Issaquah, she shopped for a while.

The following day she, the bride, and her fiancé approached Becki's car on their way to the bachelorette party when they heard the mournful mew of a kitten. Listening for the cry, they stooped to look under the car. "I don't believe it!" Becki cried out. "It's our kitten!" There in the bumper was Lucky, road-dusty and terrorized. Without a doubt this was the peculiarly marked calico from the litter back home.

The three cat lovers immediately launched a campaign. At a nearby pet shop, they purchased formula for the still suckling kitten. They calmed and washed the wee feline traveler and took her to the apartment where Becki introduced Lucky to the bride's two cats. Despite the distraction of rescuing Lucky, Becki and bride arrived on time at the bachelorette party.

Indoor life for the outdoor kitten came as a great relief and a luxurious interlude for Lucky, the traumatized tourist. "The pampering she received in the next two days," said Becki, "helped her quickly forget her ordeal." The company of other cats, the comfort of pillow beds, the convenience of a litter box (far superior to sun-hardened dirt), and the affection of wedding guests eased the adjustment from bumper to apartment. "She probably would have stayed if she'd had a choice," Becki said.

As Becki drove home (with Lucky asleep in a box beside her), she remembered her previous stopover in North Bend and in Issaquah. She wondered why the kitten hadn't mewed when she made the stops on the way to Seattle. Why didn't she crawl out

Kitty Wit:
Kittens are party animals.

from the bumper? Maybe Lucky just kept thinking, *Get me to the church on time!*

Life often takes the youthful on journeys where they never intended to go. Worse yet, their own unwise decisions can lead to frightening outcomes. Though Lucky's trip was long and bumpy, her destination offered her a slice of indoor life and the added perk of fellowship with indoor cats. Despite the misdeeds of the young, God demonstrates his mercy with undeserved benefits and well-taught lessons.

The Tail End:

White cats, particularly those with blue eyes, are predisposed to deafness. If you suspect your cat is hearing impaired, ask your veterinarian for a test. A deaf animal is vulnerable to danger because its defenses are compromised.

Becki is a para-educator working with special-needs children. She is married, has a son and daughter, and enjoys scrapbooking. Although she presently has no cats, the neighbor cats visit frequently.

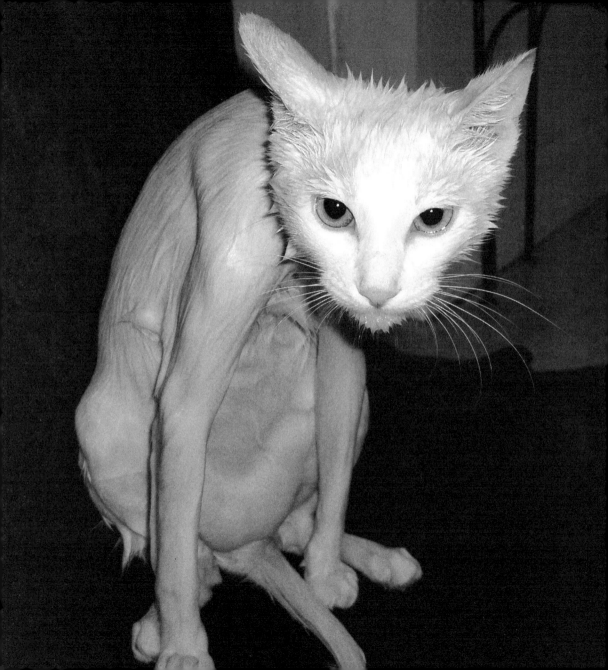

The Icy Ponds of Life

He rescues and he saves; he performs signs and wonders in the heavens and on the earth.

—Daniel 6:27 NIV

PURR-rayer:

Dear God, when others are in trouble, help me refuse self-protective ways and be quick to act.

A near tragedy in the winter of 1999 gave Randy Griffin pause. Four paws, in fact. Randy, office manager at Kryder Veterinary Clinic, tells about the fish hobby that made her a "second responder" and privileged her with saving a life.

"For some years I've enjoyed ornamental fishponds in my backyard," she wrote. "Koi and goldfish reside in my aquatic pools. The hobby has given me a lot of pleasure, including participation in the local pond tour."

Randy also fed two feral cats that came regularly to drink from her pond.

With the threat of seasonal freezes, Randy takes measures to protect the fish. Harmful fumes emitted by decaying vegetation can be fatal for the fish. Randy places a pump at the water's surface to act as a bubbler to prevent ice from forming. But the procedure intended to spare the fish was disastrous for one inquisitive cat.

"Though Midwest winters in the late nineties were mild with less than usual snowfall, 1999 was different," said Randy. "In January, four feet of snow kept me shoveling and snow-blowing almost daily."

One Sunday was no exception. After clearing the driveways in the morning, she returned to more snowfall later that afternoon. "But I noticed my clean driveway. 'Wow,' I exclaimed to my friend Tandy, 'wonder who plowed me out?'"

The neighbor that Randy suspected didn't answer the phone, so she told his wife, "Thank Jerry for me and tell him he's wonderful!" Moments later Jerry called back. He wanted her to know that his neighborly gesture provided an additional surprise for her—a surprise that stretched far beyond snow removal.

He said, "Hey, Randy, I pulled a soaking wet cat out of the snow bank next to your pond. For lack of a better idea, I left it in your garage."

Randy hung up and ran. Her experience at the clinic had prepared her for the ordeal ahead. "With temperatures above freezing," she explained, "a wet cat will lick itself dry and survive. But not at ten degrees Fahrenheit!

"Spread-eagle on the garage floor lay the body of Mom Cat, my favorite feral. I supposed she was dead. Her fur was caked in snow and ice balls, and her open eyes were fixed. When I touched her eyeball, she didn't blink. I groaned as I ran my hand across the frozen fur. 'The *poor* thing,' I muttered.

"To my surprise, Mom Cat moaned. My hopes quickened. I slid my hands under her stiff body and loosened sticking fur from the frigid concrete. I raced indoors and ran lukewarm water in the bathtub. Holding her head above water, I gently placed my little wild kitty in the water. A tumble of thoughts and emotions charged my optimism.

"In twenty years I've seen numerous animals that were overheated, but never had I seen a frozen cat. Her tail was straight as a broomstick. Minutes later, she stopped breathing. After a few chest compressions I heard a sudden gasp. While adding warm water, I continued rubbing her sides.

"An hour later, she was paddling her legs and

> ### Kitty Wit:
> Cats are like children.
> They leave their toys everywhere.

blinking." The violent shivering—evident for a while—also lessened. Randy toweled Mom Cat with firm strokes to stimulate circulation, and then reached for the blow dryer. Her tortbie-mix tresses had never been so clean or fluffy.

"I'm lucky if I catch this feral femme once a year to give her vaccines. So I really wondered what she thought of the forced bath, the Turkish towels, and the whirring, sultry breeze from the blower.

"At last I held a dry, squirming, caterwauling cat attempting to crawl across the bathroom floor. I called the clinic twice and left messages for the clinic vet. With my house thermostat set on high, I waited in the warmest part of the living room with the bundled cat on my lap waiting until Dr. Lacopo returned my call.

"When the phone rang, I jumped. 'What more can I do, Mike?'"

"You're doing everything right," he assured her. "Just keep her warm." The shivering indicated her internal thermostat was running again. For the next two hours Randy held Mom Cat until she stopped trembling and began fighting to go free.

"I moved the cat carrier from the porch to confine her indoors for the night," Randy said. "The next morning I took her to work for a thorough exam. With thankless spite, Mom Cat asserted her revival by biting the doc and drawing blood to prove her vitality. 'Not a thing wrong with her, Randy. You saved her life,' he said."

Was she grateful? "Not at all," said Randy. "She complained about her confinement with incessant meows." Until spring, unhappy or not, Randy kept her inside. Mom Cat sulked under the bed, though food, water, and litter box provided residential ease.

To prevent a repeat of the mishap, Randy placed a shallow heated birdbath in her yard and keeps it filled with water for thirsty cats.

Rescue efforts are laudable and often fueled by sacrificial love. They demand effort and optimism. Randy's neighbor was the first responder, but it was Randy's skill and affection that revived the nearly frozen cat.

Every day God deploys strangers, friends, relatives, neighbors, and professionals to save lives. Not all rescues require death-defying acts. More often, the crises of life are of a non-mortal nature. Ordinary people are capable of helping. Never overlook an opportunity to lift someone from the icy ponds of life.

The Tail End:

The words of the famous hymn, "Rescue the Perishing," were penned by blind American lyricist Fanny Crosby.

Randy enjoys landscape gardening and reading. She has a parrot, three dogs, and five cats, and says she hopes none of them ever takes a winter dip in the pond!

Opportunity Ajar

Ask and it will be given to you;

seek and you will find;

knock and the door will be opened to you.

—Luke 11:9 NIV

PURR-rayer:

Dear God, give me boldness to press firmly on doors of opportunity and daring enough to examine the prospects.

Drop-in child care, walk-in hair salons—unscheduled arrivals have become acceptable in business.

Kitty, a tawny tabby with white paws, nose, and mouth paused outside the front door of The Flower Cart in Niles, Michigan, and dropped in. Shop manager David Coquillard happened to notice the cat's unsolicited entrance.

The sympathetic shop owner, Phil Hurlbutt, allowed the walk-in to hang out for the afternoon among the fresh flowers, clay pots, and seasonal decor. Kitty tiptoed through the inventory of bouquets, vases, planters, and gift items. Was he purposely demonstrating his suitability for a store filled with perishables and breakables?

The drop-in cat continued his walk-in visits. He became known as The Flower Cart kitty, aka F. C. Kitty, and assumed permanent residence at the business. Kitty soon made a vocation of smelling the long-stemmed roses.

From the beginning, he appointed himself as greeter, sprawling in the sunlight at the shop's fragrant entrance. Regulars at The Flower Cart seldom walk past him without stroking the stripes of the feline doorman.

Though his days are mostly pleasant, life is not always a bouquet of posies. Like the day he was cat-napped. A job applicant who was refused the opening at The Flower Cart returned to the shop disgruntled and vengeful. When Kitty went missing, clues pointed to the jobless man.

Kitty's disappearance prompted citywide attention. Police were summoned, posters were distributed, and a feature story appeared in the *Niles Daily Star*. Flower Cart patrons worried and its employees grieved. After a week of Kitty's absence, hope diminished.

Three days later the shop marquee posted the news—K-I-T-T-Y I-s B-A-C-K. Dirty, thinner, and exhausted, he had found his way home. A few days of recovery and he resumed his routines.

Among various habits, Kitty stays busy in the parking lot running off canine intruders. On dull days he appreciates a joyride—one time on board with a UPS driver and once with Henry, the wholesale plant supplier. Kitty made an unnoticed leap into Henry's truck and rode to the next destination. At the final stop of the day, Henry discovered Kitty relaxed amid greenery in the bed of his truck. It was not a happy spectacle for Henry the cat hater.

Looking for excitement on another boring day, Kitty hopped onto the backseat in the car of a Flower Cart customer. When the woman pulled into her garage, Kitty announced himself with a jump to the front seat. The astonished driver was not amused. How could Kitty have known she was allergic to cat dander?

> ### Kitty Wit:
> President Calvin Coolidge once invited friend from his hometown to dine at the White Hou: Concerned about proper table manners, the gu decided to copy everything that Coolidge di Their strategy succeeded until coffee was serv The president poured some coffee into his sau The guests did the same. Coolidge added sug and cream and his guests did the same. The Coolidge bent over and placed the saucer of coffee on the floor for his cat!

"Kitty offers a happy diversion for children accompanied by parents," said Hurlbutt. "His relationship with customers earns him Christmas cards and gifts." Many come to visit Kitty when there is no occasion to purchase The Flower Cart's signature arrangements. One patron brings his elderly mother only to pet Kitty. While placing their orders, people frequently inquire about the longtime boarder. A smiling teen once asked, "Is that the same cat who was here when I was five?"

Even the employees marvel at F. C. Kitty. He never nibbles a stem, a leaf, or a petal. Floral deliverer Barb Kietzer spoils Kitty with handcrafted catnip toys. After business hours Barb returns to the shop to call Kitty indoors for the night. Annually, she takes him for his veterinary checkups. "He also stays at *my* house," said Barb, "when he's recovering from ailments."

Kitty will never be sorry he dropped in. He could have passed by The Flower Cart while presuming, *Fur and flowers don't mix.* Instead, he nudged the door open and found a good home.

Possibilities for life await our investigation. Not all we expect is behind every door, but certain passages will lead to fulfillment. God gives us signals by leaving doors ajar. It is our responsibility to explore opportunities that suggest His providence. One such assessment led F. C. Kitty to friends, forays, and fame.

 The Tail End:

Worse than the sound of a slamming door is the regret of wishing, *If only I'd knocked.*

Phil Hurlbutt, owner of The Flower Cart, is president of the Niles chapter of Civitan, an organization that helps children with developmental disabilities. He also provides all flowers for the preliminary contest in the selection of Miss Michigan for candidacy in the Miss America competition.

No Kiddin'

And He will turn the hearts of the fathers to their children and the hearts of children to their fathers...

—Malachi 4:6 RSV

PURR-rayer:

Dear God, make me mindful of the children around me and keep me in touch with their needs.

Without the cats, life for Herman could have been lonely.

His mother was ill with Hodgkin's disease and often recovering from surgeries. His father, almost fifty when Herman was born, kept long hours on the cattle ranch with Herman's elder brother and the hired men. The nearest neighbor was five miles down the road, so eight-year-old Herman had plenty of solitude.

Though Herman's sister spent time with him, the barn cats were his most reliable playmates. Always at his beck and call, they were a constant source of companionship and drama as he witnessed the scope of feline life from birth to death. He watched females nurture numerous litters and cunningly dodge predators, *most* of the time. Horned owls, coyotes, and bobcats threatened their proverbial nine lives.

During the bitter winters of eastern Washington, Herman left holes in the haystacks by arranging the bales to provide cover for the cats. Sometimes the strategy backfired. Raccoons, skunks, and bobcats discovered the warm shelters and established households of their own, sabotaging the cats.

Some of Herman's cats were friendlier than others. A few favorites, one in particular, found its way to his heart.

One stormy morning during Christmas school break, the hired hands drove the truck from the barn, and set out with over 140 bales of hay for the cattle. The load was destined for the feed racks in a back pasture six miles away. From the porch, Herman watched the heavy snowfall and the drifts form with alarming speed while the cattle waited for feed. Chains on the tires of the truck increased the chances that the men would arrive safely and return. But as the burdened lorry rounded the last curve of the driveway, Herman gasped when he saw his favorite female tabby cringing in fear atop the tall load of hay.

"Dad and the crew got home around three o'clock that afternoon," Herman said. "I'd been certain someone would see the cat when they unloaded and bring her home. But they hadn't noticed. I pleaded with Dad to take me back to the feed racks to rescue her. He was exhausted from working in the storm all day and the sky was darkening.

"Fretful and foolish, I jumped on my bicycle to hunt for my lost cat. But Dad saw me set off down the road, followed me, and then let loose with a scathing reprimand. Though he laid down the law about me staying home, he promised we'd go search for her in the morning.

"I hardly slept that night. Tossing and turning, I considered the temperature, the predators, and the

> ### Kitty Wit:
> With nine lives to expend, it's no wonder that cats are not in a hurry to wake up.

disorientation of a whiteout. My worries gave me little hope that we'd find my cat.

"First thing the next morning, Dad kept his word. With no mention of breakfast, he led me to the pickup. 'C'mon, son, we'll eat when we get back.' Crashing through dozens of snowdrifts, we headed for the pasture.

"At the base of an eighty-foot bluff, the feed racks formed a large circle, one-hundred-fifty feet in diameter. My eyes roved for an orange cat against the bleak landscape. Dad turned off the engine, and I scrambled out of the truck. No cat was in view. Evidence of fowl and animals stoked my fears. Tracks of pheasant, rabbit, and coyote imprinted the snow.

"Then a cry. 'Dad! Did you hear that?' He didn't. But a second mournful meow sounded from the nearby bluff, and there, about halfway up the face of the cliff, we saw a snow-frosted cat. Cold, scared, but alive.

"'Kitty! Git down here!' I yelled. We called and cajoled, but she paced restlessly and continued to cry. Terror impeded her desire to leave the hillside. Dad grew impatient with her reticence until we spied coyote tracks in the snow everywhere around her safe perch. Though pursued, she had found a sanctuary that was inaccessible to the coyote. I knew she was a smart cat, and at that moment I felt pretty proud of her wise standoff.

"Eventually, she started downhill. After a cautious descent to level ground, she bounded toward us, sinking in the snow after each leap.

"I don't know who was happier, the relieved cat or me. But she didn't get off without a scolding. I scooped her up and gave her a lecture similar to the one my dad gave me the previous night. She stayed in my lap all the way home.

"After that incident," Herman remarked, "it seemed that Dad was more sensitive to things I considered were of earth-shattering concern. As I've grown older, I realize the vital importance of paying attention to what is going on in the mind of a small child."

Growing up on an isolated ranch with a kind but busy father left an indelible lesson on Herman's heart. "My five-year-old nephew is now being raised on the ranch in these same channel scablands," Herman said. Sensitive to his childhood memories, Herman gave this advice: "We'd better stay on our toes."

 The Tail End:

What feeling is so nice as a child's hand in yours? So small, so soft and warm, like a kitten huddling in the shelter of your clasp.

—Marjorie Holmes

Herman is a cattle-ranch owner with a BS in agricultural economics. He serves on county and state boards in matters related to the control of noxious weeds.

You Rang?

*Let the wise listen
and add to their learning.*

—Proverbs 1:5 NIV

PURR-rayer:

Dear God, make me appropriately assertive in seeking to expand my competence by seeking specialized training and by learning from my observations.

Between South Bend and Kalamazoo stands a three-story Victorian residence in the small town of Dowagiac, Michigan. At one time, the stately home was graced by two cats,

Bogey and Shambles. The favored pair may have been the only two in the Midwest who announced their intentions to enter and exit their home by ringing doorbells.

Though neighbors marveled at the novelty of paw-operated bells installed for the cats, in the minds of owners Joan and Don Lyons the kitty convenience was not an extraordinary convention. Joan's mother had trained her family cats and dogs to use doorbells when Joan was a child. The tradition continued.

"The bell system was set up inside and out," said Joan. "My eighty-two-year-old mother still installs doorbells for both her dogs and cats. When I was a kid, we owned a summer cabin on a Canadian island, where we let our husky roam free. Mom trained the dog to open the screen door from the outside by pulling on a wooden spool, letting go, and then running indoors before the door swung back and hit him. Dad got a big kick out of telling everyone how Mom demonstrated on her knees and with her mouth in order to teach the dog."

The cats, Bogey and Shambles, also benefited from Joan's heritage. Teaching them how to use a "door bell" took about three weeks. She hung a small cowbell at the end of a rope. With cat's paw in hand, Joan would strike the bell and then open the door. Gradually, she required more independent action from the cats. When Joan noticed the cats standing at the door, she waited until one of them rang the bell. Success was always rewarded with praise.

After Joan and Don enclosed their back porch, the previous bell was inaudible. So Don installed an electric doorbell at floor level. A small knob on a wooden paddle acted as a depressor for the doorbell button. A little instruction, like pressing the cats' bodies against the paddle, paid off. The cats quickly caught on to Pavlov's principle of cause and effect.

But there was a downside to Joan's successful tutelage. The cats insisted on an immediate response after they rang. If Joan or Don were not prompt, the cats rang and rang the bell.

Near her back door, Joan had a feeder for the squirrels. While they nibbled sunflower seeds and watched the cats, the squirrels also caught on to the doorbell sequence: ring bell and owner arrives at door.

Soon after, a series of strange occurrences began. The doorbell rang but no cats stood waiting. After one such incident, Joan noticed the empty squirrel feeder. Mystery solved. The squirrels were notifying their supplier by pushing the clapper!

> ### Kitty Wit:
> Speaking of his departed wife, Gracie, and Willie, his cat, George Burns said, "Willie is temperamental, but we understand each other. laughs in all the right spots. Of course, Grac was always the number one cat in my life.

One audacious rodent, however, pushed the perimeters of Joan's generosity. The squirrel waited for her to answer his summons and when she opened the door to refill the feeder, the bushy-tailed genius ran indoors.

Joan expected the squirrels to accept her handouts but demanding more seeds with a rush on the kitchen was unexpected chutzpah. Joan's earnest investmen in doorbell education had opened doors for both cat and squirrels.

For the cats and the squirrels, specialized instruction opened new passageways in life. Likewise for people, advancement in most fields seldom occur without more training. If you hope to branch out in your career, ask a friend in a similar profession to coach you. Or enroll in a course of study to update your knowledge. Obtain licensing or certification. Register for a seminar. Consult a professional, request a mentor, and read current texts to sharpen your edge. Boost your qualifications with advanced training and increase your chances for promotion.

 The Tail End:

Second to Bogey's bell-ringing prowess, he was crowned Mr. Catsopolis in 1999. The title and trophy are awarded annually in the tiny Michigan town of Cassopolis (named Catsopolis during the days of celebration) at the 2,700-acre estate of Ed Lowe, deceased inventor of kitty litter.

Joan and Don Lyons own and operate the Heddon Museum of fishing tackle in Dowagiac, Michigan, where Joan's husband is also the mayor. Joan is writing a reference book about the Heddon fishing tackle company that began in Dowagiac in 1902 and moved to Arkansas in 1984. Heddon is acknowledged as the inventor of the first artificial fishing lure.

Hooray for the Birds

All a man's ways seem innocent to him,

but motives are weighed by the Lord.

—Proverbs 16:2 NIV

PURR-rayer:

Dear God, search my heart at the depth of my motives and keep me from actions that are driven by wrong reasons.

Herself, a young and hopeful calico, discovered a bird's nesting box under the eaves of a garden shed. When a female barn swallow also discovered the ready-made home, the elements of drama materialized—danger, dedication, and duty. The outcome of the play between cat and bird is a reminder that pure motives pay in rewards.

It all began when Mike Williams decided at last to part with the giant birdcage his deceased father had used to breed cockatiels and other exotic birds. He removed the nesting box that was mounted in the birdcage and kept it for sentimental value.

Mike and his wife, Beth Ann, Herself's people, donated the birdcage to a church garage sale to raise money for a woman in need. He offered the cage at a bargain price of forty dollars and hoped for a quick sale. A happy customer bought it, and the proceeds were given to the mother of the single-parent household. Mike said, "I knew Dad would be pleased."

After hanging the small nesting box from the eaves of Beth Ann's garden shed, he thought little more about it until he noticed his cat, Herself. She was scheming.

The nesting box with its stick perch was for rent among the bird populace in the Williams' backyard, though it didn't appear that Herself could reach it. Mike enjoyed watching a winged resident quickly occupy the box and begin the construction of a mud bed for her eggs. It was an idyllic picture except for one hazard: Herself was at large. Mike continued to keep an eye on the activities around the shed.

Herself found a way to the rooftop and poised at the edge. With hind legs straddling the roof peak and head bowed over the eaves, she had an overview of the swallow household. Though the nesting box was out of paw's reach, Herself kept a daily vigil. One can hope.

Soon the nest was noisy with cheeps from a clutch of songster swallows. Mother swallow hunted for insects and returned with nourishment for her brood. When she flew from the box, she swooped downward before making her graceful ascent. When she returned, she approached from below, evading the space between the rooftop and eaves.

The watchful cat was confounded by the swallow's aerial maneuvers. Undaunted by the constant peril of the pussycat, mother swallow routed her entries and exits in the marginal space under the ogling eyes of the cat. Life moved forward for the swallow family despite the large and hovering threat.

In nature's time, the nestlings matured, took flight, and joined colonies in new neighborhoods.

Herself had been a front-row spectator to the birth, nurture, and departure of the fledglings, but her instinctual intentions were flatly disappointed. Mother swallow had remained vigilant in her

> Kitty Wit:
> To find the best chair in the house,
> just look for the cat.

commitment to responsibility. Her motivation to protect the lives of her brood outwitted the motive of the cat.

Fortunately, even for humankind, not every devious plot is fulfilled.

Motives can be identified and corrected by looking deeply at what drives a goal. Introspection is friend to the pure of heart. Ignoble objectives often backfire, but a noble incentive always pays the reward of integrity.

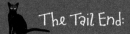

The Tail End:

According to statistics from the Cat
Fanciers' Association for the year 2006,
the top ten cat breeds rank in this order:
Persian, Maine coon, exotic shorthair,
Siamese, Abyssinian, Ragdoll, Birman,
American shorthair, Oriental shorthair,
and sphynx.

Entrepreneurs Mike and Beth Ann
Williams have retired to a fifty-hour
workweek divided among plant sales,
ceramic production, ribbon printing,
rental management, and curbing design.
Pretty, their newest cat, supervises all
their home-based business ventures.

The Dangers of Paws-sessions

Every good gift and

every perfect gift is from above.

—James 1:17 KJV

PURR-rayer:

Dear God, creator and owner of all things, help me loosen my grip on the gifts you loan me.

When Mark Burton's parents placed a black Burmese kitten in the arms of their three-year-old son, the cat claimed the boy as his own. Young Mark was not the first person or thing that Sam would refuse to surrender. Sam kept a paw on his possessions. In fact, the word *yield* was not in his vo-cat-ulary.

Mark's mother did a fine job of parenting, but apparently, Sam failed to notice. He quickly assumed the role of guardian. Sam's protective nature was as plain as the sun at noonday. When Mark got a spanking, his mother faced two protesters—a misbehaved son squirming to get free, and a protective kitten biting her ankles.

Around the clock, Sam and Mark were together. By night Sam slept with Mark, and by day he acted as bodyguard, especially against the neighbor's dog.

The seventy-five-pound mutt reveled in barking at Mark and chasing him for sport. Sam was no stranger to the feisty mongrel, whose shaggy bangs matched his witless style of amusement.

One day the feckless dog chased Mark into the backyard and up the porch. Sam's favorite place was on a chest freezer beside the back door. As Mark darted through the door, Sam leaped from the freezer onto the dog's muzzle and raked off a piece of his nose. The loud commotion broke the silence of the summer afternoon as the yelping dog ran home.

Lest the dog lose another chunk of nose, the owners tethered him to a tree. Every afternoon Sam circled the tree and harassed the hound until he was wound around the trunk like a string around a yo-yo.

Sam's possessive nature was matched only by his boldness. Though he was raised on generic-brand dog chow, he also liked people food. Sam was partial to vegetables, but he could pack a tuna sandwich. One sunny day Mark's mother served lunch outdoors. The cheeky cat carried off Mark's sandwich and ate it sooner than Mark could spell m-i-n-e.

Sam maintained property rights as well as table rights. He liked to sleep in the twenty-foot locust tree that served as his post in the front yard. While stretched upon an angular limb, he slept through everything except the sound of intruders. Whoever set foot on the lawn became a target for Sam. Like an owl on a mouse, Sam would light on the caller with inhospitable intent.

One fall, Mark's father returned from a duck hunt with a few mallards and one unsavory specimen. He threw the latter to Sam and walked indoors to unlace his boots. A sudden flash of color at the picture window surprised him. A streak of blue, gold, and green feathers sailed ten-feet upward as Sam playfully tossed the expired foul.

Kitty Wit:
What breakfast cereal do cats prefer?
Mice Krispies.

The dead duck soared skyward a second time, then a third.

When a neighbor's spaniel arrived on the scene, Sam's attitude toward the duck was suddenly defensive. In a daring stance, Sam stood between the dog and the duck. After a fierce face-off, the spaniel fled. The dog's intense interest in the duck may have made Sam presume that the oversize "sparrow" was something special. Though lifeless and distasteful, the duck was Sam's possession.

We are seldom aware of our attachments until someone tries to seize them. Quick defenses reveal our fight-to-keep instincts and our feelings of entitlement.

When God puts his finger on a belonging, an expectation, a right or a dream, we sometimes react like a possessive cat. Doubting God's wisdom, we balk at surrender.

The upshot is even worse. Things that God forbids are as lifeless as Sam's dead duck. They lack enduring worth and are unsavory as well. Nothing we hold has value if God says "Let go."

 The Tail End:

Cats are less likely than dogs to visit the animal doctor. In 2001, 85 percent of dog owners took their pet to the veterinarian, while only 67 percent of cat owners did so.

Mark Burton and his wife, Leslie, are residents of the beautiful Inland Empire in the Pacific Northwest. They enjoy exploring the wilderness on foot, bicycle or motorbike. The Burtons are refreshed by spending time with family, friends, and their current feline buddy, tomcat Reilly Bartholo-mew.

When Felon Meets Feline

When did we see you sick or in prison and go to visit you? The King will reply, I tell you the truth, whatever you did for one of the least of these brothers of mine, you did for me.

—Matthew 25:39–40 NIV

PURR-rayer:

Dear God, I choose to learn from the example of a cat's best instincts by seeking out at least one lonely person for a companion.

Some of the prison guards can testify that the eighty-three-year-old Lorton Correctional Complex had been a home to cats for more than thirty years. No one seems to know how the feline population began. But the wild kingdom can be thanked for taming the hearts of dozens of convicts.

Among the approximate 77 million cats in the United States, about 500 roamed the 3,200-acre facility in Fairfax County, Virginia, when its closure began in 1999. Concerned inmates, who were transferred to other prisons, had cared for the cats.

According to the *Washington Post*, a paraplegic sentenced for murder, once known as the Cat Man of Lorton, fed the yard cats for eight years. "Every time I feed them, I learn about responsibility and understand compassion," he said. From his wheelchair he would whistle for Al, his special cat, and soon a couple dozen cats were following his motorized wheelchair. He attributed his change of heart to the cats. "Instead of taking lives, I'm trying to save lives."

A prison spokesman said, "We believe [caring for the cats] provides some kind of reform for some of the most hardened inmates." Many of the cats, like

Roscoe, Nina, Tramp, Roadrunner, and Mama, were credited as reformers.

Inmates had three designations for their cats. "Walk cats" didn't respond to anyone. "Yard cats" stayed outdoors and various inmates cared for them. "Dorm cats" wore collars and belonged to individual inmates. A few of the cats stayed in dorms in the lower-security parts. Litter boxes were not allowed, so dorm cats also spent time outdoors.

If a cat grew ill, an entire cellblock worried. When a resident from Woodbridge, Virginia, learned the prison was closing, she began a campaign to locate new homes for all the furry friends of the confined.

During her visit, a concerned prisoner met her with a single urgent announcement: "Indo is sick." The burly tattooed man was holding a gray-and-white kitten. A second man explained the kitten's symptoms. "He's sluggish, and he doesn't want to play. Can you make him feel better?" he asked the Woodbridge sympathizer.

As one inmate approached parole, he grieved. He was leaving behind his pets of eight years. "I haven't found anyone good enough for my cats," he lamented.

Sentiments like these expressed by the inmates revealed the emotional and reformatory benefits of the campus pets.

Cats do not make judgments and do not pass sentence—two likely reasons the cats fared well among the convicted at Lorton.

The inmates with their cats remind us that those serving time for ill deeds, like all of humanity, crave companionship. Furthermore, if the company of cats can mellow the heart of a felon, the visits of well-meaning people can be equally helpful.

The heart-cry for pleasant company is common to all. May we never withhold companionship from anyone who needs it.

The Tail End:

…e expression "the cat's whiskers" …eans that something is special. The …rase is thought to have originated … the 1920s and comes from the fact …at the cat's whiskers are remarkable, …deed. They act as highly sensitive and …pid-acting antennae, helping the cat …entify things it can't see.

… 2001, the Lorton facility closed …d inmates were moved. This story … based on the *Washington Post* article …ee bibliography), and information …om Internet research on the Lorton …cility.

A Litter Bit Goes a Long Way

Carry each other's burdens.

—Galatians 6:2 NIV

PURR-rayer:

Father, help me to expect blessings from circumstances which at first I approach with resistance.

Already a cat hater, Kent Newman realized his marriage to a cat owner would only intensify his feline sentiments. Though in love with Grace, his outpouring of affection stopped at her cats.

While courting Grace, Kent had survived introductions to Big Foot, a polydactyl kitten, and to Callie Calico, Big Foot's adopted sister. Introductions, however, do little in forging relationships. Kent would later learn that day-to-day support builds friendship more quickly than polite introductions.

After Kent and Grace had wed, Big Foot and Callie met Kent's gaze again and searched his eyes for some hint of affection. Discerning as they were, the cats turned away. Kent was more relieved than offended. So Big Foot and Callie continued giving homage only to Grace, their beloved mistress.

As the newlyweds adjusted to marriage, a pair of prophets became the topic of discussion one day—Elijah, who departed from this world, leaving a double portion of supernatural gifts to the younger prophet, Elisha.

Grace applied the idea of a double-portion gift as the twofold kindness that Kent could extend by *embracing* Callie and Big Foot. Contrarily, Kent viewed the gift as the double dose of grace he needed to *endure* the cats. Kent began wishing for the virtues in his wife's first and middle names—Grace and Hope. Abounding grace and enduring hope, specifically regarding the cats.

"Wisely, Grace and the cats devised a strategy," said Kent. "They launched a class with me in mind." The course title, sounding like a college requirement, clearly revealed their determination to educate him: Cats 101. Much to his mortification, the instruction was On-the-Job-Training (OJT). At first, Kent resisted enrollment in the sessions. But finally he conceeded.

"OJT with the cats reminded me of something I once heard from a ranch hand in Texas," said Kent. "One day I poked Buckaroo Ed with a question, 'If a city fellow wanted to learn about horses, where would you start him?'

"In well-worn Wranglers and barn-scarred boots, Ed shot from the hip. 'I'd give 'im a pitchfork and shovel, and start 'im in the muck.'"

Cats 101 started cowboy style—"in the muck." Kent's OJT assignment included care and cleaning of the double-size litter box. Like most humans, cats understand love when displayed in acts of service. As Kent fed Big Foot and Callie and sanitized their sandbox, they humored him with invitations to scratch their silky heads and stroke their arched spines. Slowly, a relationship began; gradually, Kent's heart changed.

As a result, Kent passed the semester of Cats 101, even with high marks, admitted Grace. However, she now laments, Big Foot and Callie love Kent more

> ### Kitty Wit:
> Dogs have masters, cats have servants.

than her. The reason's no secret. He spent time with the cats "in the muck." He tidied their litter box and affirmed them with back strokes.

God answered Kent's prayer with the virtues he lacked—grace and hope—and blessed him with a double portion of felines whom he now loves. Thanks to education gained while enrolled in Cats 101, Kent learned that a litter bit goes a long way when kindling relationships. Bonds develop quickly when we help others shovel through the rubble of their troubles. Helpful involvement may even turn double trouble into a double treat.

 The Tail End:

s one of the beautiful compensations
this life that no one can sincerely
to help another without helping
nself.

   —Charles Dudley Warner

apted from the account submitted by
nt Newman. The minister, missionary,
1 teacher is devoted to writing and to
ving as mentor to over eighty men at
rvest Home in Sarasota, Florida.

Foolhardy or Faithful?

Now it is required that those who have been given a trust must prove faithful.

—1 Corinthians 4:2 NIV

The near fulfillment of a fishing fantasy, the hospitality of an ailing friend, and a stroll through an old neighborhood added a few pounds of cinnamon to an already spicy vacation.

Throughout the thirteen years that Judy and Roger Kiser lived in Brunswick, Georgia, Roger's heart and imagination often traveled to the beautiful California Delta where he used to fish for striped bass. Elaborate vacations were beyond the limits of his disability check, even when added to Judy's wages as a waitress. So a surprise invitation from Roger's best friend was better than an expenses-paid cruise in the Mediterranean. "Come West, Roger," Danny said, "stay with Lois and me and fish the delta." *What an idea!*

Roger knew Danny was waiting for a liver transplant, so the opportunity to renew their friendship and recover lost time would be a holiday bonus. Judy and Roger pooled their funds to cover airfare and a guided fishing trip. "We were on our way," said Roger.

Dan and Lois lived on the edge of the notorious vicinity called the Airport District. Known for its sketchy residents, poverty, and crime, it was a neighborhood where strangers were resented.

Curious, Roger awoke early the first morning and decided to walk through the surrounding blocks. At the corner of Connie Way he stopped to observe the pot-hole-ridden, half-paved roadway, the trash and the mud that comprised the scenery. Little had changed in the ten years since he had last visited. Wayward teens still mingled in gangs and stole from local markets. Junk cars, worthless tires, tall piles of garbage, and a scatter of crushed cans and broken bottles arrested his attention.

Interrupting Roger's reverie was a surprise tickle on his ankle and a rub against his leg. Roger looked down to see a small cinnamon cat do an about-face and offer a second, firm rub. Instantly, he noticed the cat's injured leg. The broken limb was visibly swollen. "She was a painful sight as she dragged a dangling foot," said Roger. I picked her up and headed back to Danny's, where we gave her food and water. Added to her physical distress was the hunger she quickly satisfied with our offerings."

Roger and Danny's eagerness to relieve the cat's agony was momentarily daunted after a first call to a veterinarian. "The clinic refused to treat the stray cat, unless we accepted financial responsibility," he said. "But a second call connected us to a vet who agreed to examine her for twenty-five dollars. X-rays showed that the broken leg had been twisted and almost severed. Amputation at the shoulder was the only solution. A spreading infection would soon kill her." Ominous news for Roger and Danny.

The price tag for the procedure came as an almost equal shock: a thousand dollars—one grand not at their fingertips.

Kitty Wit:
Cats are stubborn but they aren't stiff-necked.

Judy and Roger needed time to brainstorm. Their savings were committed to the long-awaited fishing trip with no cash flow for a spendy vet bill. "We made the cat comfortable for the night and the next morning I made a second visit to the corner store. There I learned specifics about the malicious attack. Four boys had twisted the leg until it broke, crushed the foot with a car starter, shot her in the neck with a pellet gun and half buried her alive. I asked no further questions. Sickened, I went home," said Roger.

Judy and Roger dialed numerous clinics and made their appeal for the cinnamon survivor, but the vet advised them to put the cat to sleep; he believed it was a merciful recourse. Still, the boys' cruelty stirred something in Roger's soul. "I told Danny, 'If I ever accomplish anything in my life, I will save at least one thing from the Airport District.'"

With tear-filled eyes Danny said, "Roger, that's why we've been friends for so many years. You just never give up when it comes to fixing something that's broken or hurt."

Danny's words of affirmation strengthened Roger's resolve. By day's end he and Judy located a surgeon at the Modesto Spay & Neuter Clinic who agreed to amputate Cinnamon's leg at a reduced price. They sacrificed the money for the fishing trip and gave the vet a go-ahead. A barbecue restaurant contributed fifty dollars, and Roger's son pitched in another hundred. A friend already laden with surgery debts graciously donated one hundred thirty dollars. Later, when Judy and Roger returned to Georgia, the caring folks at Delta Airlines waived the seventy-five-dollar charge for animal travel and gave Cinnamon a gift pass home with her new family, the Kisers. Roger said, "For Cinnamon, it was 'Good-bye, Airport District!'"

Recalling the experience, Roger said, "I still wonder at Cinnamon's risk-taking on that day she approached me. She chanced an introduction to a stranger on the same perilous streets where she had endured brutal acts at the hands of humankind. But the risk saved her life."

Risk calls to both the foolhardy and the faithful. The foolish take risks that produce little more than thrill, prestige, and attention. But the faithful take risks with the expectation that God will intervene to uphold a good cause. The odds are not against us with God on our side. For the faith-filled, nothing is impossible.

 The Tail End:

I dwell in possibility.
—Emily Dickinson.

Numerous stories by Roger Dean Kiser are published in the *Chicken Soup for the Soul* series. He is an orphan-survivor of a troubled childhood and youth, turning bad experiences into good by becoming a voice for abused children and animals. Learn more on his Web site at http://www.Geocities.com/trampolineone.

Cat Hater Recants

Do not judge,

or you too will be judged.

—Matthew 7:1 NIV

PURR-rayer:

Dear God, deliver me from the arrogance of unfounded and arbitrary judgments.

Monica Ackerman made no attempt to soften her opinion. "Cats are sneaky, inscrutable, and unteachable," she said. "They're wild things that don't come when you call and who care nothing about you except as food purveyor and litter pan janitor.

They are the rulers; you are their subjects. A dog, now, there's a pet. You are the leader of his pack, his reason for living."

Such was Monica's favoritism toward dogs and her bias toward cats when she was raising her children and a dog. But the years passed, the kids moved away, and the dog died.

On a sunny March day in California, Monica became a mother once again.

She stepped outside and noticed a movement in the herb garden. Behind the parsley she saw a kitten, and another, and two more. A fifth scampered behind the watering can.

To her dismay, a tribe of feral cats was living in the backyard. They dug in the flower beds, swiped lunch meat from the picnic table, and posed a general nuisance. Monica presumed the kittens were the offspring of a gray tabby she had seen trespassing.

Lest they unpack their mittens, she had no recourse but to remove them from her property. She sneaked up on the tangle of gray-and-white tabbies and gingerly dropped each one in a box. They returned her icy sentiments with scratching, squirming, and hissing.

The hands-on work was done, until she spotted a sixth kitten shivering in the shade of a bench. *Not more,* she thought. Plop, into the box! The little black kitten joined his five striped siblings.

Monica phoned her newlywed daughter and pleaded with her. "You surely have six friends. Each one could take one." *Simple math,* thought Monica. "I'll deliver them myself. Today," she said.

But her daughter offered only one-sixth of a solution. "I'll take one," she promised, "if you raise it until we move into a house."

"Why I agreed is still a mystery," said Monica. She drove to the shelter, where she supposed the kittens would find homes with cat lovers. A volunteer examined the littermates one by one, commenting on their sex after each inspection, "Girl, girl, boy, girl."

"What's the sex of the black one?" Monica asked. "My daughter wants just one."

"Boy," she said flatly, "and he's crawling with fleas."

Just what I need—fleas in my car, on my clothes, in my house. She hated fleas almost as much as cats. But she kept the black runt and waited until Monday to take him to the vet. Though tolerable as "a cute little kitten," he would soon belong to her daughter, Monica reassured herself.

After the visit with the vet, the charcoal kitty got a name: Maxx. He became the focus of Monica's days. She bottle-fed him and treated him for fleas. He slept on her chest or under her chin. Maxx traveled

> ### Kitty Wit:
> Cats are independent. They don't listen, they do[n't] come when they're called, and they like to stay o[ut] all night. When they're home, they like to eat wh[en] they want to eat and then be left alone to sleep. [In] other words, every quality that a woman hates in [a] man, she loves in a cat.—National columnist an[d] veterinarian Dr. Marty Becker.

with her and listened to the music she played in her car. Soon it was obvious that Maxx, also, was a fan of Mozart.

Though her daughter kept visitation rights, Monica objected to the way she handled Maxx and her insistence on chasing him when he didn't want to play. Monica was surprised by her own possessive reaction, which led to further questions. *What are these mother instincts? Am I becoming protective of this cat?* Her growing fondness was hard to suppress.

In three months Maxx had fully won her affections and quickly gained status as her main man. Now he runs the house, greets her at the door, licks her hand, plays fetch, and checks on her at night.

Monica's daughter and husband have resigned themselves to their loss. Monica dismissed them with the comment, "Maybe a feral will show up in *your* backyard."

From the window sill, Maxx watches several outdoor kitty-cousins who wander through the yard. They notice Maxx, too. Perhaps they covet his indoor comforts. Monica tells Maxx how fortunate he is to live inside with her. But when she gazes into his amber eyes, Monica knows she is equally fortunate.

All it took to convert a cat hater to a cat lover was a few months of fur-to-flesh contact. Nearness dispels misconceptions about animals, like one-on-one relationships diffuse unfair judgments of people.

A season of side-by-side interaction may dramatically adjust an unfavorable opinion of another human being. Typically, judgments soften and attitudes change after time, and experience helps us acquaint ourselves with those we once criticized. Be careful. Whom you judge harshly today could be your best friend tomorrow.

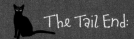

The Tail End:

Plants have inspired catlike names such as Pussytoes and Cat's Whiskers. The Star Tulip, also called Cat's Ear, was named for its hairy petals that suggest the wispy fur inside a cat's ear.

Monica Ackerman lives in the San Francisco Bay area with her two cats, Maxximus and Chelsea. She owns and operates a paralegal business that assists people who represent themselves in court. Monica's two adult children live nearby, and a three-year-old granddaughter is the delight of her life.

For the Love of Lily

Praise be to the God and Father of our Lord Jesus Christ, the Father of compassion and the God of all comfort, who comforts us in all our troubles...

—2 Corinthians 1:3–4 NIV

PURR-rayer:

Dear God, I am grateful for the unique ways you heal my wounds and renew my zest for life.

Heartbreak happens, and Debra Rinaman has seen her share of it.

The death of her father and subsequent divorce from her husband were almost enough to shatter her life. But a puff of lilylike kitten made the difference between depression and recovery for Debra.

When her twenty-five-year marriage ended, she moved from Syracuse, New York, to Spokane, Washington, to relocate near her family.

Laden with emotional trauma, decisions surrounding the purchase of a home, and the necessity of finding employment, Debra slogged through momentous adjustments. Human help did wonders, but she needed more.

Debra had always loved cats. Frankie, her gray-and-white shorthair cat, was left behind with the ex-husband. She had started her westward journey with another cat in tow, a Maine coon named Murphy, but he became ill en route and was returned home to resume life with Frankie. All that Debra cherished was now as distant as the New York city she left behind.

After a brief time living with her mother, Debra began a house search and soon settled into a new, big, and lonely residence. But her transitions climaxed blissfully when she answered an ad for Himalayan kittens.

"My sister and I were to meet the breeder at a Mexican restaurant halfway between our two towns," said Debra. She smiled and added, "It was Nepal intersects Mexico, you might say.

"I took one look at the kitten and told my sister, 'She looks like a flower.' She was my Lily." At only eight weeks old, Lily lived up to the reputation of Himalayans. "They're reputed to be gorgeous," said Debra.

"My heavy spirit lifted as soon as I laid eyes on Lily," Debra said. "Months of stress vanished the moment we united. The combination of her marble-blue eyes, white body, and gray face was breathtaking. She's the flower of my life."

Each night when Lily hears the garage door rise, she runs to the mudroom door. "I look forward to meeting her gaze after a long day on the job," said Debra. "Her companionship is critically important to me. She sleeps on the pillow opposite me; she just keeps me going."

But the kitty's antics also keep Debra on alert. "I tell friends that the Mexican restaurant where we first met must have made Lily hot and spicy!" Lily's fascination with candlelight reminds Debra of one hot night. Three scented votives were burning on the stovetop. Debra never supposed that Lily would go near. "Suddenly I smelled the peculiar odor of singed hair. I jumped up and Lily ambled in front of me. Her fur was smoldering. Luckily, her thick coat and my quick response

> ### Kitty Wit:
> We once had a cat named Joseph. We asked vet to neuter him, but he suggested *she* be spa We now have a cat named Josephine.
> —A tale of truth from a neighbor.

saved her skin from burns. I sure learned a thing or two from *that* fire show!"

Lily's attraction to the refrigerator also poses a threat. "She thinks nothing of hopping on a shelf," said Debra. "Maybe she's looking for salsa!"

After shopping one day, Debra unloaded the groceries, some into the cupboards, and some into the refrigerator. Later she began the ironing when it dawned on her that Lily, her usual tagalong, was not at her heels. Debra began a hunt that ended at the refrigerator. Asleep on a shelf, Lily was chilling out. Debra told her coworkers, "Maybe her secret ambition is to be a popsicle!"

Debra prefers that Lily entertain herself with her favorite low-budget toy. A satin ribbon cut from Debra's nightgown exceeds the pleasure of all the high-tech toys, pet-catalog specialties, and catnip mice among Lily's selection of playthings. "She's no different than the kid who'd rather bang the cupcake pans than beat the fifty-dollar drum Grandpa bought at the toy store," said Debra.

Playtime was not fun for Lily on one fateful day. When she was twelve weeks old, she nearly hanged herself. Debra was in another room when Lily began dragging a feathered cord around the house. When Debra heard the strange noises of fumbling, scratching, and gurgling, she followed the sounds to the living room and found Lily in a stranglehold. Both owner and cat were gasping for breath before Debra could free Lily from the noose.

Debra contends that Lily is worth her occasional calamities. "Her sweet, inquisitive, and loving nature is what makes her who she is."

In the two years after Debra moved west, her life took a refreshing turn. "The support of my mother and sisters, my work at a medical practice among a nurturing staff, and the affection of Lily are responsible for averting a bout of depression that would likely have followed my midlife divorce and the loss of my father. I'm especially grateful for the love of Lily."

The sincere and well-intentioned ministrations of friends and family may fall just a whisker short of healing the deepest wounds of a bereaved and broken heart. But a God-sent cat is sometimes the God-sent balm that soothes the soul.

 **The Tail End:**

The Himalayan breed is prone to tear overflow. To avoid eye infections and staining of the fur, "Himi" owners apply a wet, warmed washcloth, once daily, to wipe the clear or brownish liquid from their cats' eyes.

On weekdays Debra is happily employed at a family medical practice. Walking is her favorite recreation. On weekends she frequently entertains her nieces and nephews and is host for their sleepovers.

Mews-eum Security

Each one should use whatever gift he has
received to serve others,
faithfully administering God's grace
in its various forms.

—1 Peter 4:10 NIV

PURR-rayer:

Dear God, thank you for the ways you use us that originate from the endowments with which we were born.

Vaska doesn't carry a gun or wear a security badge, but he earns his keep along with fifty other guard cats at the Hermitage Museum in Saint Petersburg, Russia.

In 1764, Catherine the Great began the display of the museum's world-renowned collection that now includes three million pieces of artwork. The empress also chose a selection of cats to keep the building free of rodents. The tradition of cats has continued because of their success as mice exterminators.

Two employees care for the community of cats that live in the basement. They are barred from the main floor exhibit halls lest they damage a canvas or leap on a pedestal, but they stroll through the gardens in the summertime.

Vaska is the eldest of the cats. The twelve-year-old sentry pushes his basement boundaries by sneaking into one of the four hundred halls of masterpieces. Vaska's favorite destination is The Pavilion Hall, which houses the elaborate gilded Peacock Clock. Maybe he remembers the rhyme

about the mouse that ran up the clock.

The deputy head of the museum's supervisors said, "He usually does it on Mondays, when the museum is closed to visitors, and unnerves the museum's security, who have to rush into The Pavilion Hall when Vaska sets off the alarm system."

As troublesome as Vaska can sometimes be, he's not the only cat around the museum. The facility's felines present challenges simply due to their sheer numbers. A caretaker for the corps of cats said, "The Hermitage does not have enough mice and rats to feed all the cats. Hence, they dine on fish, chicken liver, porridge, and canned food twice a day."

Though the Hermitage cats are neutered, their populace still grows. People know that the museum employs cats as in-house predators, so they either abandon them on the museum property or bring them in when their owners die.

Regardless, the Hermitage cats do not forget their main duty. The purr-suit of rodents is their mission. By simply doing what is instinctual—hunt mice—the Hermitage crew of stealthy guard cats fulfills a role that serves both the arts and its patrons.

Like Vaska, each of us has a failing. But we are smart to remember that the natural fact of being whom God made us, and accomplishing what we are best suited to do, enables us to perform a service like no one else.

 The Tail End:

The earliest known domestication of cats began when they learned to coexist with humans after their capture as predators for controlling vermin in Egyptian granaries.

One might say that the Hermitage cats are owned by the museum staff and all its visitors.

Surviving and Thriving Post 9-11

Give everyone what you owe him . . .

if respect, then respect; if honor, then honor.

—Romans 13:7 NIV

PURR-rayer:

"Bless the beasts and the children. For in this world they have no voice. They have no choice."
—Barry Devorzon and Perry Botkin, Jr.

Arthur was homeless soon after the collapse of the World Trade Center on September 11, 2001. The twenty-pound, black-and-white cat was the pet of New York Fire Captain Marty Eagan, Jr., who died during rescue efforts.

Skip Kellner, the director and chief counsel for the Suffolk County, New York SPCA, described Arthur as a special case among hundreds of saved pets. Arthur lived with Eagan's mother. After 9-11, Eagan's two children moved to their grandmother's home on Long Island. But one child's allergy forced a sad outcome: five-year-old Arthur had to leave.

When pet owners perished in the debris of the Twin Towers, hundreds of Manhattan dogs and cats were abandoned in apartment buildings. A California couple, Derek and Robin Latour, read a news article about the homeless pets. Without delay, they sent an e-mail inquiring about the possibility of adoption, hoping to add an orphaned animal to their family of two dogs, three cats, and a turtle.

Kellner said the SPCA faced difficulties relocating Arthur. "People are funny. We got calls offering to take a 'black Lab' or a 'Boston terrier,' but not many willing to take just any pet. Then I remembered Robin's e-mail." Numerous gestures of goodwill ushered the now famous feline to his new family on the western seaboard.

For starters, American Airlines donated the first-class ticket for the transcontinental flight. Arthur was the first among pet survivors to travel cross-country to a new home. "Interestingly," Robin said, "my great-grandfather, Major William Robertson, was one of the founders of Robertson Aircraft, which was a precursor to American Airlines."

Adding to the benevolence of American Airlines, a second gesture of support came from PETCO, who gifted the Latours with a year's supply of cat food.

Like Robin's connection to the airlines, her husband had a remote link to the cat's original owner. Derek's grandfather—like Captain Eagan, Jr.—had been a fire battalion chief.

Squad Sergeant Robert Galoppi served as Arthur's escort for the cross-country trip. Days before, Galoppi had been treating cracked paws and the dusty eyes of dogs that assisted in the search at Ground Zero. Galoppi also rescued two cats from a pizza parlor. "It makes you feel good that you're doing something," he said.

Animal lover Robin Latour, 32, is a natural stepparent for Arthur. She gravitates toward needy animals. While at college she saved a laboratory rat that was destined as supper for a snake. At other times she rescued a lost dog in the desert, saved a

> Kitty Wit:
> Cats are softer than software
> and never require an upgrade.

turtle from certain death, and adopted a kitten she heard mewing in a trash bin.

Following the introduction to Robin, Arthur relaxed in her embrace and rested a paw on her arm. She said he felt "squishy." Afterward, she commented to journalists, "I'll put him on a diet."

One year later, when the rock band U2 performed during halftime at the 2002 Super Bowl, a running list of 9-11 victims was projected on a screen behind the band. Robin and Derek watched until they saw Captain Eagan's name. "It's weird how you can feel so connected to someone you never knew," Robin said. She believes their adoption of Arthur was meant to be.

Arthur prefers routine. "He's not an adventurer,"

she explained. "And he keeps a schedule to catch the best sun rays. At ten o'clock I can find him in one spot, at eleven o'clock in another."

Robin is quick to praise her cat. "Arthur is fantastic," she exclaimed. "He waits for me to come home, and I know he's going to greet me when I start down the walkway."

Robin paused to remember those early days. "He's mellowed quite a bit. When we first took him home, he was feisty," she said. "He cohabits well with our two female cats, but he favors Daisy Mae, our sixty-pound dog. He likes to walk between her legs and press against her stomach."

Arthur's history, post 9-11, traces a long trail of honor. The staff at Suffolk County SPCA honored the memory of the valiant Captain Eagan, Jr. by finding the best home for his cat. Tireless 9-11 volunteers honored the lives of other deceased and missing owners of surviving pets, and cared for search-and-rescue dogs that worked to find trapped and injured humanity. The path of honor then wound its way to northern California to the home of the Latours, who honored Arthur with their enthusiastic adoption.

The Tail End:

Who sows virtue reaps honor.
—Leonardo da Vinci

Derek is a research scientist pursuing an MBA, and Robin is in Private Equity at Credit Suisse. They are passionate about traveling, and when not enjoying soccer, cooking, or gardening, they just like to "hang out together."

The Cosmopolitan Cat

All nations will come and worship before you,

for your righteous acts have been revealed.

—Revelation 15:4 NIV

PURR-rayer:

Dear God, deliver me from an insular attitude and swell my heart with inclusive love.

A fictional sailor, a busy butcher, and a homeless cat are the key players in a multicultural story that teaches a universal lesson. It all began with a trip to the animal shelter.

When Steve Egger, a butcher of Austrian descent, visited the Spokane Humane Society to adopt a cat, he handled several contenders before selecting a wee gray fellow. "I like this one," said Steve, "but he's not very active," he remarked to his wife. The others climbed and squirmed.

"No sooner had I said 'not very active,'

73

than he jumped on my shoulder and crawled around my neck," said Steve. "I was impressed. He understood English!"

Home went Steve and Diane with a shelter cat of dubious pedigree.

A good name for a male should be strongly masculine, thought Steve. So he named the cat Sinbad after the central character in the folktales about a Persian-born sailor who made adventurous voyages to fantastic places. The Austrian butcher now owned a cat that understood English and had a Persian name!

a purebred, the vet said his mixed lineage surely included a Korat queen or stud.

Now, the Austrian butcher owned a cat that understood English, had a Persian name, and was of Thai descent!

The colorful ethnicity of Sinbad's story contains a global truth. At every turn in life, we intersect other races that enrich our own. God is the Maker of all. Though governments delineate borders and racial prejudice divides, the love of God is boundless. He embraces the world and excludes no one.

> ### Kitty Wit:
> If cats competed in sports,
> they would undoubtedly choose freestyle events.

Like all responsible parents, Steve made an appointment with the vet for Sinbad's vaccines. The veterinarian's observation added to the international flavor of Sinbad's adoption. After examining him, he shared this conclusion. "Steve, this cat's from Korat stock. The exotic breed originates from the province of Khorat, a plateau in Thailand."

Steve exclaimed, "But, doc, he's a shelter cat!" He felt pretty lucky having adopted a cat with exotic genes.

The vet described the features of a Korat: gray coat, eyes with a green center and amber edges, a stocky build, lavender paws, a slight break on the nose, and no undercoat. Though Sinbad's white paws and double coat disqualified him as

In general, Italians care less for dogs but find cats charming and companionable. Thousands of cats live in the Forum, the Colosseum, and other historic landmarks in Rome.

Steve Egger is the son of a large family that owns and operates four meat markets in Spokane, Washington. Steve and his wife visit some of the seventy-five lakes within fifty miles of Spokane to participate in summer fun, especially boating. Sinbad, now seventeen years old, vacations with them in the family trailer and houseboat, and even goes for an occasional cruise in the motorboat.

Stealing Hearts at the Lighthouse

Let your light shine before men,

that they may see your good deeds

and praise your Father in heaven.

—Matthew 5:16 NIV

PURR-rayer:

Dear God, keep my light burning even in the bleakest of nights.

Can curiosity really kill a cat? Ask Bruno. The orange, long-haired tabby climbed the spiral stairs to the lantern room of the Heceta Head Lighthouse and insisted on inspecting the top of its 205-foot tower. Like sightseers at the lighthouse, perhaps Bruno wanted to view the ocean from the unique vantage above the waves. After all, he lived with the light keepers. Didn't he deserve entrance to the lighthouse itself?

Fearful that the gears would mortally

injure the snooping cat, the keepers notified the Coast Guard and turned off the light. A prompt reply from the Coast Guard officer contained nothing of a maritime concern. His anxious response amounted to three words: "How's the cat?"

"Okay," the light keeper replied. He stopped the gears in the nick of time and escorted the unharmed feline back down the stairs.

Both Bruno the cat and the lighthouse are named after Portuguese Captain Don Bruno de Heceta of the Spanish Royal Navy, an explorer who passed along the Oregon coast around 1775.

One day after Bruno's trip to the tower top, the friendly cat disappeared for good. Lighthouse innkeepers Michelle and Steven Bursey suspect that one of the many tourists who visit the lighthouse may have cat-napped the handsome kitty.

Another of the lighthouse cats, Don, was also named after the famous sailor, Don Bruno de Heceta. But a gender discovery mandated a new spelling for Don. When the cat's growing midriff produced a litter of kittens, Don became Dawn. Since Dawn also lived at the light station, her new name, D-a-w-n, seemed like a fitting change—dawn, sunrise, a bright light, a lighthouse. You get the drift.

The Burseys host many year-round guests who come to the magnificent Oregon coastline to tour the lighthouse, twelve miles north of Florence, and to lodge in the home of the original light keepers. The restored white, two-story Queen Anne house, included in the National Register of Historic Places,

serves as a bed and breakfast inn, and is home to Dawn and another cat, Marley.

No strangers to comfort, Dawn and Marley laze in parlor chairs or doze on the front porch of the *circa* 1894 keepers' house. On the porch visitors gather every fifteen minutes, waiting for their tour, or they sit and admire the cats. "Everyone fawns over Dawn," said Michelle.

As Dawn mingles among the tourists, she schemes for attention. Available for gentle strokes, soft words, and ear massages, she works the crowd. She escorts each group into the house and then

> Kitty Wit:
> What do cats like best on a hot summer day?
> Mice cream.

returns to the veranda to welcome the next assembly of tourists who "fawn over Dawn."

In the mornings bed and breakfast guests sit around the antique dining room table and enjoy the Burseys' seven-course breakfast. Under the table and unseen, the cats offer hospitable shin rubs, without objection from visitors. Only once did a couple leave the Inn because of allergies to cat dander. A set of bed and breakfast rules listed on the Inn's Web site includes a notice—"No pets allowed. We have two cats who will not allow it."

The Heceta Head Lighthouse, situated along scenic Route 101, is the most photographed light station in the United States. William Britten, author of *Top Ten Lighthouses*, calls it "Oregon's Jewel." The Fresnel lens of the working lighthouse casts its beam twenty-one miles out to sea, making it the brightest light on the Oregon coast. But Michelle and Steven might disagree about its superlative description as "brightest."

"Sometimes I wonder what is *really* the brightest light around here," quips Michelle. "Dawn and Marley steal the show most of the time. Sometimes I think people forget all about the lighthouse."

Man-made structures, like lighthouses, attract attention and inspire awe. Yet living creatures, like cats and other pets, whose hearts beat softly and whose affections spread joy, cast the light of life upon the sea of humanity. They brighten the days of our lives.

The Tail End:

The "cat's paw," a mariner's term, means a light ripple on a calm sea, indicating the end of a prevailing calm. It is also a loop formed in a line or rope attaching to a hook.

Since Dawn and Marley passed away, two new cats greet the lighthouse guests— Merry, a Christmas present from the Humane Society, and Sheba, an all-black cat that showed up one spring. Steven's and Michelle's favorite part at the inn is preparing and serving their gourmet breakfast and visiting with one another and with the crew before beginning the day's other tasks. "We feel very fortunate to be able to care for the beautiful keepers' house," said Steven, "and to share it with the public." Michelle and Steven hike the many trails along the coast and also enjoy gatherings with friends and family. Steven tends a large garden behind the keepers' house, and Michelle is busy assembling a cookbook.

King of the Clinic

I urge ... that requests, prayers, intercession and thanksgiving be made for everyone— for kings and all those in authority.

—1 Timothy 2:1–2 NIV

PURR-rayer:

Dear God, help me lead with compassion when I work or serve in positions of authority.

Cats rule. Though Sam wears no crown, his imperial status is unmistakable. On the receptionist's counter at Wandermere Animal Hospital, he sits enthroned on a large appliquéd pillow.

Sam's insistence on ruling his domain earned him the boot from a previous home among multiple cats. But at Wandermere, Sam is sovereign. A sign on the front door reads, CLINIC CAT ON DUTY. He proudly presides over sick pets, concerned owners, and conscientious staff.

His majesty is a six-year-old, blue-eyed Himalayan mix. Dr. Linda Wood, resident veterinarian, says the white-and-apricot cat is partly a flame point indicated by his pale orange markings.

Food is a delicacy for the overweight monarch. It doesn't help that the fifteen-and-one-half-pound cat is capable of opening his own food tub. On weekends Sam stays at the animal hospital, supplied with a dish of rations for two-and-one-half days. Usually he overindulges on Friday night, leaving nothing for Saturday and Sunday. As a king, Sam does what he pleases.

The Wandermere clientele patronize Sam with loving homage in gifts and attention. Some drop in just to introduce Sam to a friend.

One night burglars broke into the clinic. People who heard about it later phoned to inquire about Sam. They seemed indifferent to the thievery attempt. The staff happily reported that the cat came through unscathed. However, clinic receptionist Kari Moore said, "We can only imagine how Sam responded during the break-in. It was probably something like, 'Take the cash, but don't touch my food tub!'"

Minus a scepter, Sam keeps clinic patients in line. He shows the least tolerance for dogs and adult cats. From his countertop throne, he oversees the lobby and the stairway to his bedroom. One day a boundary dispute of noisy magnitude ended when Sam cornered a large and unmannered Labrador in *his* stairwell. Sam will not be deposed.

Kings are known for their conquests. On one occasion a mouse invaded Sam's second-story bedroom, which sparked a territorial breach in his quarters. The staff suspected an outbreak of war between Sam and some critter when they spied the agitated king in hot pursuit behind a row of three-ring binders.

The next day Dr. Wood discovered the trespasser when she reached for a file and lifted a binder. The flattened mouse had succumbed to death-by-depression beneath the thick binder and the weight of the king.

Sam also undertakes to capture other intruding raiders. A stone fireplace in the lobby snares a few red-shafted flickers. No one but Sam hears the soft flutter of wings when a trapped woodpecker struggles

> ### Kitty Wit:
> It's the cat's house.
> We just pay the mortgage.

to go free. Sam alerts the personnel by tracking through the clinic halls with black sooty paws. "Hey, everybody, there's a bird in the chimney!" Someone opens the flue and soon the bird finds its way down the chimney, into the lobby, and out the front door—while Sam is confined upstairs!

Sam keeps royal tabs on every patient. After an appointment Dr. Wood asks the pet's owner to join her for a consultation in the lobby. She reserves an empty chair for Sam between her and the client. Without fail, Sam joins the session. He also participates in staff meetings and tarries until the gathering is dismissed.

Though Sam is heavy on authority, he has a soft spot for kittens. He licks, sniffs, and nuzzles their muzzles, purring all the while. Even if a feisty young thing rebuffs him, he bounces back to welcome the next kitten with interest and love.

Sam has been described as supreme commander, physician's assistant, morale officer, grief counselor, and office manager. Whatever else he is—step aside, Elvis—Sam is the king.

His desire to inform and supervise is obvious. But so is his tenderness toward kittens, their owners, and the Wandermere staff of caregivers.

Who of us hasn't known a Sam? A pompous person may behave like royalty, but an imperious demeanor could be hiding an underlying disposition of mercy. Pretentious superiors may try our patience, but they also deserve our respect.

 The Tail End:

Move over dogs; cats are power icons. In 2001, Apple Computer launched an operating system called Mac OS X Cheetah. The system was named after the big cat to connote power. Cheetah was followed by versions named Puma (2001), Jaguar (2002), Panther (2003), Tiger (2005), and Leopard (2007).

Dr. Wood, a veterinarian for 30 years, shares her life with Dunny, a yellow Lab; Buckwheat, a dachshund; Bentley, a cat; and Forest and Dually, her two horses. Dr. Wood enjoys dressage riding and spending time with her husband.

The Pusillanimous Pussycat

Encourage the timid,

help the weak.

—1 Thessalonians 5:14 NIV

PURR-rayer:

Dear God, help me encourage valiance in others by staging courage behind them with my prayers and support.

Flash earned his name by his fearfulness and speed. Always on the run, fleeing from real and imagined threats, he often cringed in shadowed corners. He feared people, dogs, and even the breeze-blown curtains.

Encounters with a formidable yellow tabby had reduced Flash to a chicken-hearted, indoor cat. But a single incident of victory changed the craven kitty from timorous to intrepid.

By the time Kari Widman met Flash, the transformed cat no longer cowered in fright. His dread of strangers, also, had vanished. The once fainthearted feline, formerly terrorized by gatherings of people, now offers cheek rubs on shins and walks tiptoe across laps. Thanks to John, his owner, Flash is free from his fears.

But it wasn't always so. Originally, poor Flash led a fearful existence, thanks to intimidation by Bully, a tough tomcat. Routinely, Bully approached the sliding glass door where Flash sunned himself. Bully's puffed-up fur and menacing stare conveyed the threat *I could beat you up!*

Flash, gray from ears to tail tip, would arch his back and jet to another room, looking like smoke from a diesel exhaust.

Kitty Wit:
Nothing succeeds like a little success.

One warm afternoon Flash lay indoors alongside the glass door when Bully sauntered up the stairs outside.

As Bully came near, Flash arched his spine and spiked his ashen fur. John stood behind Flash and decided to play the monster. With teeth bared, back arched, arms outstretched, and fingers curled like talons, John appeared ready to spring into combat with Bully, the tyrant.

The combined affront of Flash and John unnerved the bully, and he darted from view like a streak.

Surprised and triumphant—though oblivious to John's drama behind him—Flash took credit for the victory and acquired a spirit of gallantry. The newly emboldened cat began venturing outdoors with a swagger of self-respect.

John's behind-the-scene reinforcement was life-changing for Flash. One strong victory after a series of defeats empowered the cowardly cat.

Victories for humankind are often achieved in a similar manner. We help others to face their fears and regain their valor as we step in behind, or come alongside with encouragement.

Are you that giant of bravery whom someone may need?

If a friend is defeated by fear, don't hesitate to help. Be there—in a Flash.

The Tail End:

Cats keep breeding in a do-or-die effort to perpetuate the genetic strains of finicky-ness.

Kari Widman of Tacoma, Washington, has been a language arts teacher at the junior high level, a community college instructor (GED, adult basic education and developmental classes), a bookseller in a Christian bookstore, and a women's Bible study leader at her church.

No Trick, All Treat

Before they call

I will answer; while they are still

speaking I will hear.

—Isaiah 65:24 NIV

PURR-rayer:

Dear God, when my imagination fails to perceive what I need, I am grateful that your foresight has already prepared for my necessities.

Sometimes we receive without asking and find without seeking. Even so, the treasure we get is exactly what we need. A Halloween treat was one such gift for Linda Waud

and husband, Dan. God's foreknowledge of Linda's illness was the primary factor in a surprise arrival at the Wauds' front door.

On October 31, a faint cry from the porch roused Linda as she rested on the sofa. "Dan," she summoned, "more kids are here."

A dish heaped with chocolate bars sat on a tabletop. Dan opened the door. He looked left and then right. No children in costume waited on the porch.

Instead, foregoing the conventions of a proper invitation, a dainty cat scurried between his legs and entered the house. Her brisk steps and purposeful bearing left Dan and Linda speechless but smiling. A short tail and curious gait declared like a label, *I am an original.*

Contrary to Halloween myths about cats and ill fortune, this one brought blessing.

Dan and Linda were awestruck by their presumptuous guest, whose close-set eyes were azure blue. Her singed whiskers led to some guessing. Perhaps she had poked her nose in a glowing jack-o'-lantern on that annual night of the pumpkin.

Amused by the cat's unabashed entrance and engaging friendliness, the Wauds noticed an unfavorable reaction from Stanley and Abby, their two resident cats. Stanley, the elder statesman, didn't need an interloper overthrowing his thirteen-year status. And Abby, a retiring calico, found no humor in the intruder's playful advances. Abby alternated between gazes of condescension and auras of superiority.

Around 9:00 p.m., the candy was gone and the doorbell stopped ringing. But the naïve houseguest remained. "What are we going to do with her? Just set her outdoors?" Linda asked Dan.

He countered. "We have a dog, a big one at that, and two cats! We don't need more animals."

By bedtime Dan's firmness had mellowed dramatically. The Wauds could not imagine anyone, including themselves, abandoning the elegant cat with the amiable temperament and the melodious purr.

During subsequent weeks they searched for an owner and quarantined the feline caller in a basement room. When no one responded to flyers, ads, or calls, they took her to the vet. He confirmed three things: she was a seal point Siamese, approximately five years old, and free of disease. Surely, they surmised, the exotic and healthy cat had not been a vagrant all her years.

Two months later Dan and Linda began losing hope of connecting with the previous owner. By now they had given their guest the name Coco, and they considered her a part of the family. However, one day

> **Kitty Wit:**
> Cats don't celebrate birthdays;
> they commemorate lives. Nine, in fact.

Linda met an interested pet lover and invited her to visit Coco. But Dan loathed the idea of losing this cat. "You *can't* give her away." Linda could hardly miss his ringing emphasis on "can't."

Her two-word rejoinder finalized the question of Coco's future. "I know," she agreed.

Later in spring the doctor diagnosed Linda with breast cancer. Treatment began. The miseries of chemotherapy assaulted her body with gastric upset, consuming fatigue, and frequent insomnia. Psychological distress added to the side effects of the chemical cure. Daytime was barely tolerable and nighttime felt interminable. The foreboding and sinister disease with its implications of death taunted Linda.

"I spent most of my time on the sofa, sleeping whenever my body would relax. And always, Coco was there, kissing my ears with her wet button nose, licking my hair, or napping beside me. Even if I'd lie on the floor, she'd settle her light little body beside me." Even the way she walked made Linda smile; Coco took each step as if she had paste on her paws.

School reconvened the following September, and Dan, a middle-school choral director, returned to work, leaving Linda alone much of the day. "Dan was the first," said Linda, "to recognize that Coco had been sent from God." Like a nursemaid, Coco's attention was Linda's daily consolation.

But a sacred encounter would transcend even the tender ministrations of the God-sent pet. Linda discovered that Coco was only a gentle forerunner for a second and more glorious guest.

During a peak in her emotional anguish, she saw a vision of Jesus at her bedside one night. With calming authority, He assured Linda with words He had long ago spoken to his disciples. "Do not let your hearts be troubled. Trust in God; trust also in me." His bidding to resist fretfulness and to trust God infused her with peace. Sweet tranquility instantly canceled the destructive power of anxiety.

Linda had asked for neither creaturely cat nor celestial visitation, yet she received what she needed and more. Though natural fears still attempt to trouble Linda's heart, her caregiving cat and her peace-giving Lord have taught her that God will always be there when she needs Him.

 The Tail End:

Due to the malicious practices of a few people who hold superstitions about cats, many animal shelters refuse to allow the adoption of black cats during the week of Halloween. Though keeping your kitty indoors is the safest choice year-round, if your cat is an outdoor pet, always keep it indoors on Halloween and on the several days preceding.

Formerly a children's ministry director, Linda Waud is now a stay-at-home grandma. She serves at her church and in several cancer groups.

Got Cats?

Be of one mind,

live in peace; and the God of love

and peace shall be with you.

—2 Corinthians 13:11 KJV

PURR-rayer:

Dear God, in an imperfect world help me be hopeful and creative when working toward solutions for peace.

In a suburb of Spokane, Washington, a two-story house invites the attention of passersby. Its showy flower beds are bedecked with yard art in cat motif. Indoors, twelve predominantly exotic cats parade on white carpets, sharing the upscale residence with adoring owners. But when cats congregate, purr-sonalities collide. Pat Holmstead and David Dominick enforce restrictions on a few agitators that work toward keeping the peace.

In 1998 Pat and David left the harried pace of California to move with their multiple cats near rolling farmlands and stately evergreens in the Pacific Northwest.

A quintessential Birman was the first to win the hearts of the previously "dogs only" couple. They noticed a strikingly lovely cat crossing the street. "We were stunned by her beautiful blue eyes," said Pat. A neighbor said the cat had been dumped. Pat's impulses took over. "I think we should adopt her! What do you think?" she asked David. They came home with Misty the Queen, the start of their feline family.

Their second was Maxwell, a Siamese Applehead, and also Pat's favorite. "He's one-hundred percent lover," she said. But Maxwell demonstrates no fondness for feline foes.

His archrivals include Little Boy, a clever black cat who opens bifold doors with his paw, and Monty, a smoke-colored tabby adopted from Pet Rescue. But Maxwell contends for the spot as top cat. Competition among the three demands separation: Maxwell upstairs, the other two downstairs. The triangle of hostility is the only tension amid the dozen cats.

Squeaker is the noisiest of the twelve. This hefty black female has a cry that mimics Ethel Merman. Onyx, a gem indeed, is the household's other black cat.

David is both funny and fanciful when talking about Gray, their Russian Blue. "He could be an alien," David kidded. With a sardonic smile he explained. "Most aliens are gray, you know." The ash-colored cat with brilliant green eyes is an armful now, but not before his owners captured him. They placed open cans of tuna and salmon inside a cat carrier and enticed Gray from his wild kingdom. In a similar manner, they snagged Squeaker and Little Boy on separate occasions.

Squeaker was slow to adapt. For a year she hid under the bed except to eat and drink at night. At last, David attracted her with a feather-tipped pole.

When David tickled her spine, Squeaker engaged and played roughly (cat claws and blood!). Her self-imposed exile ended. Soon she was lounging on Pat's plush sofas and overstuffed armchairs.

One in the menagerie of twelve cats believed she could fly. Even as a kitten, Squirrel excelled at jumping, Pat said. "She used to make a flying leap across the bed to the cat tree." Despite all her jumps and spins, the tortoiseshell cat has never broken anything.

Squirrel, nicknamed Twirl-a-Girl, is David's heartthrob. David, also a motorcyclist, plants kisses on the heads of all his cats.

Kitty Wit:
What do you call a cat that lives in an igloo
An eskimew.

"Squirrel was my first love," confessed the mischievous David. "That is, until Kiddin' came along. I may take Kiddin' to Las Vegas and marry her," he jested. "I always like the newest cat the best. The previous beloved gets jilted."

He stroked her tricolored fur. "Kiddin' treats us like dirt, but I love her madly," David said. She fell sick with a respiratory infection two days after her adoption. Four weeks of forcing down medications had "turned her rude," explained David. The calico Kiddin', sometimes called Jennyanydots, is dotted with a large orange spot on her forehead, earning her the name of T. S. Eliot's poetic cat.

Seven-year-old Mister Munch loves to eat. David and Pat spotted him in a box of kittens while shopping at a flea market. Licking plastic is his eccentric habit.

Oversize paws and an uncommon bulk hint at his probable Maine coon ancestry.

David found Venus de Milo caught between the storm doors at his workplace. David and Pat returned at night with a carrier and bait, while Venus—Lady of the Night—was catting around. The next morning she showed up and, off guard, she entered the portable kitty kitchen.

When Pat worked at a hospital, a feral mother and kittens found refuge under the nearby Dumpster. When the transporter carried off the refuse container, the terrified mother fled, leaving her kittens in a mud puddle. A hospital housekeeper placed one of the drenched and mewing newborns in a box and delivered her to Pat, who borrowed the hospital's electric water pad and warmed the trembling kitten. Pat realized later that this cat's experiences with water—mud puddle and water pad—had left her with an affinity for water. She now drinks from water spigots and mews outside shower stalls. A favorite pastime is chewing on Pat's washed and still-wet hair. David named the kitten Spiker, after water specialist Sheri-Lee Piker, the gutsy firefighter.

These twelve cats of sundry breeds cohabit under a single roof. Amazingly, animosity exists among only three. The minor controls imposed by David and Pat keep peace among their dashing dozen.

It's usually the few, not the many, who cause unrest over rank and status in both feline and human communities. Restraints help control antagonists in society and protect cordiality among the majority. We are well-advised to remember that working at peace averts wars as well as cat fights.

The Tail End:

A biotechnology company has developed a scientifically proved hypoallergenic cat. The cat offers relief for those who sneeze, weep, and itch from reactions to the feline protein that causes the symptoms. Visit www.allerca.com.

Between the interview with Don and Pat and the release of this book, a few of the dashing dozen have dashed off to kitty heaven, a haven of purr-fect peace.

The Indictment of Indifference

A righteous man cares for the life of his animal.

—Proverbs 12:10 NIV

PURR-rayer:

Dear God, make me steadfast in my pledge to those under my care, and deliver me from the unprincipled trait of indifference.

Connie Christilaw has nursed for thirty years, but her caring nurture began years before that and has extended beyond human perimeters; she has rescued and treated many a feline. Experience saving cats has taught her that placing a rescued animal is a journey of both red and yellow lights.

In high school Connie adopted Amos, her first cat. Thereafter, she was a confirmed and fervent cat lover. When Amos was gone, big gray Jake brought Connie lots of joy. She longed for another cat. Without Jake's permission, Connie acquired Sophie, a gray-

and-white striped kitten with cotton-white paws and matching belly.

Sophie loved two things: Jake and shoes. Her infatuation with footwear kept her happily entertained, and her attachment to Jake made her lastingly devoted.

But Jake did not reciprocate. Sophie's arrival made him furious. Consequently, he was even less disposed for the advent of a *third* cat, soon to come.

During a break from nursing, Connie was living at a mobile home park. From her porch step one morning, she heard a melancholy meow. The cry led to the community center, where she spotted a tortoiseshell cat dangling from a tree limb. Seizing the opportunity, the cat dropped onto Connie's head and held on with a panic-stricken grasp.

What does one do with a cat for a hat? Suddenly, Connie was now in charge of a cat's future. Suspecting that Jake and Sophie might not be sympathetic to the hapless cat, she braced herself as she headed back to the house with a furry skullcap.

Jake and Sophie met the intruder with sharp hisses. Averting a further squabble, Connie placed the cat in a carrier. She reasoned that temporary confinement for the stray cat was safer than confrontation with Jake and Sophie. The relieved cat purred in agreement and surrendered to sleep.

After work Connie drove to a vet clinic. The electronic scan showed no microchip lodged under the skin of the collarless kitty. The vet treated her for fleas and ear mites and wrote "Fleabag" on the new patient's record. Later she became Phoebe, a name more feminine and flattering!

Of special interest in the vet's diagnosis were injuries that gave clues to Phoebe's dispatch alongside the highway near the mobile park. Torn hind toenails and lacerations on the flanks are commonly the result of a spinning fan belt whipping a trapped cat under the hood of a moving car. Had she fallen from a vehicle?

The good news was that Phoebe's virus-free blood sample approved her for a temporary stay with Connie. But Jake and Sophie were unduly threatened, and Phoebe was the object of blatant rejection, so Connie advertised her in the newspaper.

One respondent informed Connie that she drove

> *Kitty Wit:*
> A rose by any other name would smell as swe
> A cat by any other name would be an insult

every weekday on the highway running parallel to the park. Despite her inquiry, she sounded unaffected about reuniting with her cat. Yellow light number one.

They scheduled a time to meet at the vet clinic. If the woman claimed the cat, Connie would assign her responsibility for the vet bills. When they met in the lobby, Connie held forth the cat and asked the pertinent question. "Is she yours?"

The woman replied with shocking uncertainty. "I *think* it's our cat," she said. "She *might* be." Yellow light number two.

Think? Might? Could she be sure had it been her child that had disappeared? The woman's toddler seemed familiar with Phoebe. "Kitty, kitty!" she repeated. But the mother's ambiguity was indicting, indeed.

Observers in the lobby pieced together the scenario. One man furrowed his brow; another gave a discreet but negative shake of the head. A young adult rolled her eyes. Their facial expressions clearly denounced the lackadaisical response of the cat's supposed owner. Connie felt emboldened by the support of onlookers. Two yellow lights quickly turned red.

Connie hugged Phoebe to her chest. "Well, if you can't positively identify the cat, I'll hang on to her," she said.

The woman answered with a flippant, "Okay." She summoned her children and made a hasty exit. Slam bam, it was over. Didn't she care? Was she sidestepping the liability of vet bills? One thing was sure. Her indifference closed the case and the gavel fell with a judgment of suspicion.

Friends of Connie's, whose cat had just died, took Phoebe on a trial basis. A weekend invitation stretched into a decade. Many years of affection awaited her from the new owners. Need I mention that Jake and Sophie were especially pleased about Phoebe's departure?

The cool response of Phoebe's probable owner reminds us that apathy speaks loudly. Indifference may even indict us. God hates the milk-toast stance of neutrality. Jesus alluded to the attitude of noncommittal in one of His discourses. He said, "Let your 'yes' be 'yes' and your 'no' be 'no.'"

"Maybe. Kinda. Sorta." Ambivalent words will tell on you. A dispassionate attitude reveals a lukewarm heart. Indifference may also be a tell-tale sign of irresponsibility. Whether related to our feelings toward our cat or our approach toward God, fervency and devotion are the distinguishing characteristics of commitment.

The Tail End:

Deserted cats are a nationwide problem. In 2002, *The Press-Enterprise*, a southern California newspaper, reported that owners reclaimed about 1 percent of the 47,000 plus cats and kittens in shelters, and only 15 percent of cats found adoptive homes, often through rescue groups.

Connie will soon retire from her long nursing career. Gracie, another shelter cat, is her most recent rescued kitty. Connie makes beaded earrings as a hobby and plans to sell them at craft fairs when she retires. She and her husband relax by golfing and scuba diving.

A Midnight Message

Speak, for your servant is listening.

—1 Samuel 3:10 NIV

PURR-rayer:

Dear God, help me recognize your voice through messengers I'd least expect.

When Niki Anderson's mother-in-law, Goldie, was a little girl, a cat that relieved itself in her dress shoe provoked its own eviction. After the messy insult, the discourteous kitten found no welcome in the heart or the house of Goldie Anderson. But Goldie's offending first cat was not the last to enter her life.

In Goldie's elder years, her warm curiosity toward Niki and Bob's trio of feline brothers began a happier experience with cats. Goldie stroked their striped heads, held their soft bodies with her fumbling grasp, and caressed them with her wrinkled palms. In return, they responded with the soft vibrations of contented purring. One day she commented to Niki, "If I were to relive my life, I'd have a cat." It was clear; her childhood kitty had been fully absolved.

A variety of felines resided at the nursing home where Goldie lived. Elderly Sherman with his characteristic snaggletooth was a favorite. Rotund Smokey slept in the out-basket on the receptionist's counter. And Oreo strolled down the halls bringing cookie sweetness to aged residents.

As Goldie pressed toward ninety, the family planned a reunion-style birthday party and prayed she would endure for the milestone celebration. With the dawn of June 14, relatives arrived from faraway places, and she was ready for the gala.

Not long after, she suffered a stroke and failed rapidly. Her speech was slow, and waking hours were few. Slumber eased her detachment from this world, but distanced the family further from the mother they loved.

The family hoped for a surprise revival like those they had witnessed after Goldie's other serious setbacks. Following a previous illness and months of recuperation at a care center, the nurse supervisor had made a cheerful declaration. "She's strong and active! We can't keep up with her!" To everyone's astonishment, Goldie had rebounded.

But would she pull through again? Dared Niki ask God if the end was near? She withheld her question. Notwithstanding, an answer came through a cat.

One afternoon while at Goldie's side, Niki heard an insistent meow. A carbon-black cat commanded her attention. Midnight jumped onto the bed, stepped gently over the lumps of Goldie's diminutive body,

and circled in a few calculated turns before curling in repose at Goldie's feet.

What brings you to this bedside? Niki wondered. Her curiosity grew when her sister-in-law mentioned that Midnight had paid a call earlier that day.

That evening Niki, her husband, and his brother made a tearful visit to Goldie's quiet room. And guess who arrived? Midnight leaped onto the bed. She headed toward Bob, who was holding the frail, pale hand of his mother. In a gesture of sympathy, Midnight pressed her cheek against their clasped hands. Walking in step to the calming tune of her

> *Kitty Wit:*
> There is no snooze button
> on a cat that wants breakfast.

purr, she settled in a spot at the foot of the bed. All watched silently and exchanged glances, gratefully accepting the warmth of Midnight's visit.

A nurse parted the curtain partition and joined them. "I see Midnight is here again." Who could miss the attendant black cat in the solemn gathering? "She's been with Goldie much of the time," she told us. "A little black angel," she added. No one disputed the heavenly description.

Niki continued to struggle with the possibility that Goldie might leave them. Or would she? Might she rally, even yet? On the drive home Niki's mind turned to Midnight, the cat that was seemingly assigned to her mother-in-law. She pondered why it was Midnight, not one of the other cats, who came that first afternoon and began the watch-cat vigil. With sudden clarity—the reason was plain. For Mom, the hour was approaching midnight. Her heaven-going was imminent. Had Midnight given notice with her very name and her farewell visits?

Niki sighed and resigned. The clock would soon strike.

During Goldie's last days, Midnight called on her regularly when family members were away. The family, too, checked in often and whispered words of affection in Goldie's ear. A few days later Goldie departed, trading the darkness of midnight for the daylight of eternity.

When Niki returned to the care center, she had hoped to see Midnight, the tender connection to Goldie. But the messenger cat was not in sight; like Goldie, she was gone with the night. Midnight had finished her assignment, and Goldie had completed hers.

Niki remains ever mindful that God communicates in ways too numerous to count—through the admonition of an elder, the guidance of a counselor, or the visit of a messenger in furry masquerade.

The Tail End:

A nursing home administrator quoted in *Cat Fancy* magazine says, "Cats have a special way of knowing when someone is in the dying process." Oscar, a hospice cat at the Steere House Nursing and Rehabilitation Center in Providence, Rhode Island, has proved his knack with twenty-five correct calls. He curls up beside dying patients, usually four hours before their passing.

Niki describes Goldie Anderson as the dearest mother-in-law any woman could ever have wished for.

Persuaded by Desperation

Whoever is wise,

let him heed these things

and consider the great love of the Lord.

—Psalms 107:43 NIV

PURR-rayer:

Dear God, forgive my resistance to your loving entreaty.

The kitten was a wild little creature, hardly bigger than a teacup—a menacing six inches of clawing, spitting, yowling fury.

Through a peep hole in the box, Rebekah Montgomery noticed the obvious: the kitten was spunky but unhealthy. Protruding ribs and a distended belly indicated a case of intestinal worms. Her eyes were matting pus and she was infested with fleas.

Rebekah marveled at the farmer who had successfully captured the little beast and wedged her into a box. Though plainly sick, the cat was altogether unmanageable. Duly enraged with her predicament, she had no qualms about expressing indignation. At intervals, her tiny paws, fully equipped with needle-sharp claws, punctured the closed lid as she fought to get free.

When Rebekah had spoken to the farmer about a kitten for her children, she hadn't envisioned an aggressive little fiend.

She commended the farmer for his considerable effort in corralling the furry fistful of disease and fierceness. But the look in his eyes spoke volumes. He would not be pleased if Rebekah refused the incorrigible cat. She gulped and thanked him.

As the farmer set the box in Rebekah's outstretched arms, the kitten began hurtling herself, frantically feeling for an exit. All the while, she narrated her search with angry mews.

Rebekah's young children could not ignore the clamorous kitten. They pressed their ears against the box and listened to her scramble about. "Kitty is wild," Rebekah cautioned them, "so you really can't play with her, yet. You'll have to leave her alone for a while until she's tamed."

Rebekah planned to leave the kitten in the box until the busy little creature calmed down, and afterward to feed her. "Over food, you can often make friends with a kitten, even a wild one," Rebekah said. With stern warnings to each child about not touching the kitten, she set the boxed feline on the back porch and sent the children to play.

But the temptation was too much to resist for a curious cat-loving little girl. Mary, Rebekah's daughter, peeked inside the box. Seizing the opportunity, the kitten leaped straight toward Mary, bit her squarely across the bridge of her nose, jumped from the box, dashed out the porch door, and retreated under the foundation of the house.

Having escaped the clutches of evil humankind, the kitten intended to stay as far away as possible. No amount of pleading, "Here, kitty!" brought her forth.

At night, while the children slept and the kitten sang the blues—loudly, if you please—Rebekah and hubby tried to coax it by reaching under the foundation with tidbits of raw hamburger, tuna, ad nauseum—the smell of which would attract the most resistant of cats. Hoping to tame her, they supposed

> ### Kitty Wit:
> Handling a feral kitten is the purr-fect storm.

they might hasten the process if she learned that food comes from the hands of humans.

For several days kitty steadfastly refused to emerge, regardless of their offerings. Her cries grew increasingly plaintive and weak, and her appearance became more bedraggled. When anyone came near, she scampered to the farthest corners beneath the house and hid in crevices beyond reach.

One afternoon, when Rebekah had nearly given up hope, her youngest son, Daniel, called her to the back door. In his chubby grasp was the hungry kitten, fast devouring part of Daniel's bologna sandwich. Three-year-old Daniel had spent time on his elbows talking to the kitten through the foundation vents; apparently, she crawled out and volunteered to help eat his sandwich.

The kitten's full stomach made the difference, just as Rebekah had told the children. After the meal, the newcomer submitted to domestic life. Ever so meekly, she endured an eye-and-ear cleansing, a flea bath, a dose of deworming pills, and lots of enthusiastic attention from the children.

The family christened her Vivian-the-Lionhearted.

These days Vivian needs no enticements. When anyone opens the back door, she runs indoors and heads toward the nearest person. The rewards of family life offset her former desperation and persuaded Vivian to surrender her feral habits.

Vivian is like the throng of people who remain distant from God. Helpless and hungry, they hide beneath the foundations of heaven, unwilling to receive from the loving hand that feeds them. Plagued by fear and skeptical of God's outstretched arms, they cheat themselves of His gifts. Yet He waits, calling gently, and sometimes even pleading to satisfy their needs.

Persuaded by desperation, the stubborn nature gives way at last to the realization that there is nothing to lose and everything to gain. The obdurate heart yields to the gracious urging of God, and a life is transformed.

 The Tail End:

He is no fool who gives what he cannot keep to gain what he cannot lose.
—Jim Elliot

Rebekah Montgomery, a resident of Illinois, is the editor of *Right to the Heart of Women* e-zine. She has taught Bible for thirty years and is a speaker, an author of numerous books, Bible school curriculum, children's musicals, and is a prolific writer of magazine articles.

Stormy Aftermath, Sunny Outlook

Now faith is being sure of what we hope for and certain of what we do not see.

—Hebrews 11:1 NIV

PURR-rayer:

Dear God, when life leaves me desolate, turn my face heavenward lest I remain adrift on the floods of misfortune.

Clad in a painter suit, a respirator, and gloves, Rosemary Campo salvaged little more than jewelry, a bowling ball, and cat figurines from her water-ravaged home. Hurricane Katrina had destroyed her books, clothes, photos, and furnishings. Oil paintings of cats—a gift from the artist—hung in ruin, and mold and mildew clung to the home's flood-battered structures. Even so, seeing past the disaster, Rosemary's hopeful outlook shaped her emotional future.

In August 2005, when city officials ordered residents to evacuate New Orleans, Rosemary's son, Charles, drove his mother to nearby Hattiesburg, Mississippi, for a two-day stay. But the levees broke, dashing their plans of a speedy return.

One thought relieved the seventy-eight-year-old widow. Though a lifelong cat lover, when Katrina struck Louisiana, she owned no beloved cat to search for, or worse yet, to leave behind.

"After four days in Hattiesburg, I told Charles, 'We have to get out of here.'" The winds were snapping tree limbs like they were twigs, and an intolerable heat wave followed. "I've never been so scared in all my life," she said.

She and Charles drove 2,400 miles north, to the home of her younger son, John, in Washington State, and waited for information from insurance companies and FEMA, and for government sanctions permitting their return.

Her sons tried to spare their mother the televised films and descriptions of Katrina's devastation. As floodwaters peaked, even her car floated in the garage. Snapshots of the house, sent from Rosemary's granddaughter, verified her sons' fears. Rosemary would never again reside on Paris Avenue.

Nine weeks after the hurricane, she, John, and Charles revisited the brick house where Rosemary had lived for forty-five years. "It was worse than I ever imagined; like a war zone," Rosemary said. They rummaged through wreckage looking for belongings. Rosemary even searched for her bowling ball. "Of all the things you want, Mother, why that bowling ball?" asked John.

"I made him root and root until he found it," she said, smiling.

Rosemary's fondness for cats led her to a beloved collection, sodden in the deluge. Displayed on a shelf under her television, fifty cat figurines stood covered with fungi. Only one was damaged, and another was missing. Some had been presents from her husband. They symbolized the imperishable memories of life at its best.

"My husband was a cat lover, too," she said. "Ninety percent of our cats were strays. Our calico, Mary Ann, went missing for three weeks. Every day John called me from work and asked, 'Did Mary Ann come home?' Though John was the most business-minded man I ever knew, he left his job at midday to go get that cat the day she was found!"

Having feared they would never find her, he vowed, "No more cats. Losing them is too hard."

Days later, John softened his resolve. Seeing an advertisement for kittens, he called the breeder. The sole kitten remaining was an all-white runt. Rosemary named the wee fur ball Antoinette and confined her indoors. The regal feline lived to be twenty. She and Mary Ann died before the wrath of Katrina had an opportunity to sweep them away.

> ### Kitty Wit:
> Rule #1 in *The Cat Owner's Survival Guide*:
> Know your place.

Reflecting on her assortment of figurines, Rosemary concedes, "They aren't valuable in a monetary sense." They are a cherished mix of gifts, keepsakes, and souvenirs. Two favorites include a small, clear, glass cat with a smaller kitten visible in her tummy, and a miniature five-piece set of a mama cat with nursing kittens.

The inanimate collection reminds Rosemary of the live cats beside her when her sweetheart since grade school, John, Sr., died suddenly at fifty-three. Three days before his heart attack, the couple learned they had been victims of a scam. Worsening her plight, Rosemary was strapped with a hotel mortgage. Indomitable, she accepted her obligations. For the next seventeen years, she and one son ran the family's mom-

and-pop hardware store and paid off all creditors.

Rosemary's sons and her cats brightened the years. She recalled a happy event in her home. "One night at a card party, a lady helped clear the dessert dishes. Astonished, she called to me from the kitchen. 'Rosemary! There's a cat sleeping in the sink!'" On hot Louisiana days, Antoinette stayed cool in the stainless-steel enclosure.

Six months after the hurricane, Charles settled permanently in the Northwest, and Rosemary assumed the lease at his renovated apartment in a New Orleans suburb, where she preferred to live. "I just count my blessings," she said. "I have my family and a roof over my head."

Resigned to not owning a cat, she won't take the chance of losing one to a storm.

One time during Rosemary's ordeal, she had wept and said to herself, "I just hope God gives me the strength to live." That hope is reality. She now attends events at a Catholic parish where she eats lunch and plays bingo at senior gatherings.

"Some nights I get a crying jag when I think of all the beautiful things I lost," she confessed, "but I think of friends who still have no places of their own." Though smitten with brief spells of shock and heartache, Rosemary's outlook is positive. No hint of acrimony sours her story. Something as large as the support of her sons and something as small as a cat figurine continue to buoy her spirits.

Experience taught Rosemary that a God-ward outlook keeps you afloat. When villainous storms rage, we can look inward upon our losses or upward to our Helper. The direction of our focus will sink our emotions or point us toward a Lifeline.

 The Tail End:

Veterinary Pet Insurance (VPI) of Brea, California, is the nation's oldest and largest licensed pet insurer. In 2005, its active policies accounted for 60 percent of the pet insurance market.

When Rosemary relocated to the apartment, John added to her collection of figurines with a set of bamboo cats from Bali, and Niki gave her a cat of leaded crystal.

The Advent of Marshmallow

And God said, 'Let the land produce living creatures according to their kinds . . .' and God saw that it was good.

—Genesis 1:24–25 NIV

PURR-rayer:

Dear God, I am often deceived by the glitz of consumables. Keep reminding me that people, plants, and pets are always more valuable than material things.

Though sweet, round, soft, and white, he's not the marshmallow you pierce with a stick and roast over a campfire.

This Marshmallow is a white cat whose weight matches his girth—twenty-seven pounds by twenty-seven inches. The swinging cat door is a hazard; he can't pass through or even back out. DeeAnn Sylvia, his mom, dislodged him after the first attempt. The vet mandated a diet, but Marshmallow wasn't hearing it. Maybe he supposes his immensity balances nicely with his noticeably short tail. Who understands the rationale of a cat?

But Marshmallow's ongoing gift of himself is as big as his belly. He's the living version of the slogan, "The gift that keeps on giving." He is also a good mouser and a lover of family. Though he loves the Sylvia children, his best friend is Sadie, a golden retriever. Marshmallow even mimics the wagging style of Sadie's tail—side to side like a rudder.

Unlike the typical, limber feline, Marshmallow is clumsy at grooming. His hind paws don't reach past his midsection to relieve itching ears. But no *body* is perfect.

These many years later, a snapshot of Marshmallow serves as wallpaper on DeeAnn's office PC. Her desktop at Life Center Foursquare Church is arrayed with an assortment of cat figurines, mugs with cat quips, a cat-themed calendar and a collage of kitty pictures that tout her affinity for felines.

Marshmallow made his first appearance at the Sylvia home two days before the holidays as he scavenged for scraps beside the garbage tote. DeeAnn gave him a can of cat food, all 5.5 ounces, which he quickly devoured. Inspired by the handout, the vagabond cat devised a plot.

"That Christmas, Marshmallow arrived as the best of presents," said DeeAnn. "He presented the gift of himself."

Pretending to be a gift, he returned on Christmas Day like the postman's delivery of a holiday package. DeeAnn, not inclined to refuse the hungry, welcomed him to the family's traditional Christmas feast. The dispossessed cat showed no reluctance accepting an invitation to the banquet.

Four sons and two other cats, Spot and Eunice, already resided with DeeAnn and husband Randy. Their previous cat, Oscar, had recently died. Therefore, Randy was adamant about limiting the household's populace of pets. He wasn't ecstatic about Marshmallow's visit. However, he couldn't help notice how their young son, Zachary, delighted in the four-legged refugee.

DeeAnn soon concluded that Marshmallow was a stray. The previous summer the neighbors had posted an ad describing the "Found Cat," although no one responded. For days Marshmallow hung out on the neighbors' porch and passed the time studying their

> *Kitty Wit:*
> For the homeless cat,
> Christmas Eve is a boring night.
> "Not a creature is stirring, not even a mouse."

parakeet through the window. Marshmallow rolled in the dirt while they gardened, and strutted about when they entertained.

The time had come for DeeAnn to appeal to Randy for Marshmallow. Deductive reasoning was her first strategy. "Randy," she began, "Eunice is just not affectionate with Zachary like Oscar." Randy was stoic.

For a second strategy, she tried sympathy. "I *really* miss a lap cat!" She pleaded in a tone that touched on the emotional.

Randy has no recollection of sanctioning the adoption of Marshmallow. But the cat stayed, and Randy can't forget it, especially at bedtime. The supersize cat with the amber eyes sleeps with DeeAnn and Randy, and he snores . . . the cat, that is.

The family has learned a lot since the Christmas of "Marshmallow's Advent." Though no white elephants were exchanged that December, one white cat just keeps on giving. The memory of toys and jewels and tools are now as forgotten as the wrapping paper that adorned them. No one recalls the trinkets or treasures. But the big soft cat, who presented himself to the family, remains the best gift ever.

Selecting gifts can be a bane of the holidays. Before buying, we ask ourselves, *What gift would be lasting? What will most satisfy?*

The Sylvias know the answers to those questions. Living things are the best things—like a tree that keeps on growing, or a plant that keeps on blooming, or a cat that keeps on giving.

 The Tail End:

Domenico Scarlatti's Fugue in G minor is named "The Cat's Fugue." The melody originated from Scarlatti's cat. Having leaped upon the master's keyboard, the cat "struck a random and unlikely series of notes, out of which the composer fashioned his fugue."

The Sylvias are full-time staff members at Life Center Foursquare Church in Spokane, Washington. Randy directs men's outreach and recovery ministries, and DeeAnn is the nursery director. Marshmallow appears to have failed on his diet and still avoids the swinging cat door.

Venue for Teatime and Cat Lovers Alike

Whatever your hand finds to do,

do it with all your might.

—Ecclesiastes 9:10 NIV

PURR-rayer:

Dear God, engage my energy and ignite my heart for the labors to which I am called.

Dawn Kiki cradled a bone china teacup after serving fruited tea and petit fours. "I've been a cat lover all my life," she said. "I also love elegant things like fine linens, flowered dishes, and dainty foods, and I find pleasure in serving."

Dawn's self-description is a cameo of the petite proprietress and hostess at Brambleberry Cottage & Tea Shoppe. Her servant heart and feminine flair blend with her deep sympathy for the numerous cats she inherited with the 1906 Victorian cottage, home to her business of gracious events.

The sign on the teahouse omits the mention of cats, but the feline factor plays prominently at Brambleberry Cottage. Fancy boxes of teas line the shelves. High tea is observed four days a week. But cats, some named after the specialty teas, stroll on the lawns, cavort between shrubs, and jump the iron fence surrounding the cottage. Lady Grey and Gunpowder, among others, roam the cottage gardens.

When Dawn and her mother, Melanie Lenhart, moved the Tea Shoppe to Brambleberry Cottage in downtown Spokane, Washington, they acquired the parade of feral cats. The kitties were not a disappointing surprise. Dawn, a cat fancier herself, had shared her family residence with a Birman cat for thirteen years.

An iron gate laced with vines of morning glory marks the entrance to the nineteenth-century cottage. A flowered walkway leads to a picture-book porch where the cats sleep undisturbed on pillowed benches, as hats-and-gloves-clad customers arrive and depart.

Besides high tea, other offerings at Brambleberry Cottage include painting classes and gift and collectible shopping. The ongoing baking of scones also provides "make it and take it" fare for buyers hosting socials of their own. Hence, in addition to competing as a premier destination for high tea, the Tea Shoppe is part bakery and part cattery.

The nine-room house includes four tearooms furnished in a pleasing mix of antiques, shabby chic, and twentieth-century decor. In the largest tearoom, named Lady Rose, the walls are scripted with quotations from the Bible and from classic poets like Robert Browning. A selection of teas, generous sandwiches, savories, scones, and desserts delight palates during the service of high tea.

The cats, however, are not allowed indoors. Though barred from the house, they offer a furry patchwork on the grounds. Casualties from a neighborhood in transition, the stray cats once lived with former low-income residents. When the previous homeowners moved elsewhere, entrepreneurs attracted to the charm of the old district set up shops. Sadly, departed neighbors have resulted in deserted cats.

Dawn's goal is to feed, neuter, and find homes for them. She neutered Gun Powder, a green-eyed black male, and others. Another adoptee among the original thirteen strays was Momma Kitty, a six-toed Siamese

> **Kitty Wit:**
> When you're speechless,
> let your tail do the talking.

mix, and the first cat Dawn domesticated. "At first Momma Kitty was a contrast of friendly and skittish. Eventually, she let me pet *all* her kittens," said Dawn. "That's a supreme compliment from a feral queen," she added.

Momma Kitty was the most refined of the Brambleberry cats. She loved teatime. After her eviction from the previously empty house, she seldom stopped yowling to come inside. One day an employee heard a faint mew in the kitchen. However, none of the staff had seen a cat underfoot.

The case of the mysterious mew was eventually solved—but not in the kitchen. A woman seated at tea in the dining room asked to borrow a lint roller to remove some cat hair. "Remove *cat* hair?" questioned the hostess.

The elegantly groomed guest explained, "We're enjoying your cat. We've passed her from lap to lap as we've sipped our tea."

Not everyone is fond of the teahouse mascots. One woman arriving as a guest of friends was put off by the cats in the yard. She refused to come farther. Her friends rushed indoors and asked, "What should we do? We didn't know she was afraid of cats." The experienced staffmember had the perfect solution and hurried to the porch. She clapped her hands and sounded a "bizz-bizz," and the cats scurried from sight.

Despite an occasional objection to the cats at Brambleberry Cottage, they take credit for reversing a few attitudes among the feline phobic. One former employee, previously averse to cats, adopted a Brambleberry female and her kitten. A student in the painting classes had despised cats, but her observations at Brambleberry converted her to a cat lover. She now owns over a dozen.

Who knows what the future holds? One of the tearooms may someday be reserved for those who desire the company of cats, and another for those who disdain them. When seating her customers, Dawn could ask, "Cats, or no cats?"

As administrator, baker, hostess, caterer, and kitty caregiver, Dawn invests both labor and love. Toil inspired by passion endures as her distinctive combination. The amalgamation of hard work and heartfelt devotion will turn a midday meal into a feast. Effort and ardor applied to almost any endeavor promise the laborer a fine result.

The Tail End:

In the Victorian era, high tea, which included meat, was served about seven o'clock at a high dining table rather than a low tea table. Low tea, a light afternoon meal, included a tray of scones, tea sandwiches, savories, sweets and tea, and was served at a low table. Most teahouses in America use the designation of high tea to describe the ultimate in afternoon tea service.

Dawn Kiki also operates a custom painting business, and as time permits, she participates in mission trips with her husband Kelly. After the couple participated in short-term missions through Hope 4 Kids International, Kelly founded Tools 4 Schools, an organization that raises money for impoverished schoolchildren in Africa.

Taxicab Chauffeur

Let your conversation be always full of grace, seasoned with salt, so that you may know how to answer everyone.

—Colossians 4:6 NIV

PURR-rayer:
Gracious God, free me from the discourtesy of suspicion when others show curious interest in my life.

Two cats, a New York couple, and a chatty cabbie made national headlines in April 2007. They taxied 2,500 miles from New York to Arizona in a canary-colored SUV cab. The novelty of a long-distance move in a taxicab seized international interest that reached France, Colombia, and Australia. Cats Cleo and Pretty Face were part of the media obsession, complete with pa-*purr*-azzi.

Like many New Yorkers, Bob and Betty Matas were not drivers. After a day of shopping in Manhattan, they hailed a cab. The conversation led to the Matases' upcoming retirement in Sedona. The cabbie asked so many questions that Bob thought he was nosy. In jest, he asked, "Do you wanna take us?"

"Sure!" said cabbie Douglas Guldeniz.

Rather than transport their cats in an airliner cargo hold, they paid Guldeniz a reasonable fare of $3,000, plus gas, food, and lodging. Betty rode in the taxi and Bob rode with the driver of the U-Haul truck, filled with their belongings. The cats were chauffeured in the taxi, each in a carrier with water, food, and litter pan. Cleopatra, a calico, and Pretty Face, a Birman, took some extra-long naps.

Bob and Betty had purchased Pretty Face, a purebred show cat with masklike face, at the Madison Square Garden cat show. "The monks worshipped Birman cats centuries ago," said Bob. Since his incompatible housecats live in separate rooms, maybe Pretty Face thinks she's a goddess.

The New York *Daily News* followed taxi and truck for the duration of the trip. On the day of departure six cars waited outside the Matases' Forest Hills home in Queens. "Photographers elbowed one another and clicked pictures as we loaded the vehicles," said Bob. "NBC even called and asked if we'd leave with an entourage from Times Square." Bob answered politely, "No, but thank you."

Once on the road, the Matases received frequent cell-phone calls from television and radio stations. Walkie-talkies facilitated communication between Betty and Bob. In every state people asked, "Are you the New Yorkers with the cats moving to Arizona?"

"When we drove through Tennessee, a police car tailed us," said Bob. A taxicab with a New York license plate aroused suspicion. "But the officer pulled ahead, smiled, and waved us on," he said. Word was circulating to law enforcement agencies about the unique caravan.

At nightfall the cats lodged in hotels with the Matases. Bob and Betty ate dinner with Guldeniz, interviewed with a staff writer from the *Daily News*, and posed with the cats for a tall blond photographer. A full account aired on evening news and appeared in various newspaper dailies across the country and on television.

> ### Kitty Wit:
> When cats think "green,"
> it's all about catnip.

Though cat-apulted to fame, Cleo and Pretty Face took breaks from their celebrity exposure. In the mornings they hid in a corner of the hotel room or on boards under the mattress. But the tolerant cats never meowed in the taxi.

After days of travel the Matases with their two cats pulled into Sedona. The president of the Sedona Chamber of Commerce had arranged for a police escort from Flagstaff to a parade ground in Sedona, where Mayor Pud and a large gathering waited with a TV satellite truck. Townspeople lined the streets, waving at the convoy of cab and U-Haul. "A truck occupied by a dozen New York photographers were snapping away," said Matas, in his matter-of-fact tone.

"I was flabbergasted with the reception," said Bob. He asked the mayor, "Do you usually have this turnout for people who move here?"

"No, not exactly," she quipped. Attendance

outnumbered the greeters at Jackie Onassis's arrival years earlier. But Jackie hadn't arrived in a taxi with a pair of cats.

The city also hosted a luncheon with city officials and a three-day stay for the Matases at the Hilton Hotel. The cordial welcome included flowers, champagne, and colorful books about Sedona.

The hotel manager invited a photographer from the *Sedona Red Rock News* for a photo shoot of the cats. Afterward they enjoyed a reprieve from their cages at a pet boarder's. Amid all the fanfare and special treatment, Cleo and Pretty Face may have noticed one faux-*paw* at the hotel—no salmon appetizers on the room-service menu.

Bob said the hoopla continued. "We got calls from *The Tonight Show with Jay Leno* and Ellen to fly out for their shows. And when we went uptown, shopping in Sedona, a French lady in a boutique recognized us." Her sister in Belgium had faxed her copies of articles reporting the story.

The six-day trek of two seniors drew unusual attention; some say it was a human interest story. Cat lovers may say differently. The feline component stimulated just as much interest as the humans.

The public's gracious reception of the Matases made the interruption of privacy and the unforeseen festivities a pleasant experience. We can never predict when the spotlight may shine on us. To cooperate in an amiable manner is more commendable than the sudden honor or the celebrity status. Genial behavior is the best response to unexpected recognition. Take your good manners even one step further. Relax and enjoy the limelight.

The Tail End:

For interstate travel, or travel to a neighboring country like Canada, have your vet examine your cat, and obtain a health certificate prior to traveling. If you cannot produce a certificate at border crossings, you will be held up while you answer questions.

Bob is a former audio/video director. He worked for NBC filming a missile takeoff at Cape Canaveral, and for the *Tonight Show Starring Johnny Carson*, and conducted multimedia presentations for tuxedo events at the Ritz-Carlton. Betty, a retired executive administrative assistant, passed away some months after the move to Sedona.

At Home

He who dwells in the shelter
of the Most High shall abide
under the shadow of the Almighty.
—Psalm 91:1 NIV

PURR-rayer:

Dear God, I feel lost. Guide me back home. Amen.

In small town Coloma, Michigan, once called Dickerville, people no longer dicker for goods. Like cats, money is no longer scarce.

Chicago residents drive one-hundred miles to spend cash at Coloma businesses. They vacation at resorts on Paw Paw Lake, or they summer in handsome second homes and in condos along its eleven miles of beautiful shoreline.

The Eye of the Beholder antique store in a nineteenth-century house, along with an adjacent workshop, occupies two of Coloma's yesteryear buildings—so do two cats that live in the house.

Sebastian Shoup built the workshop in 1876. He handcrafted wooden boats and grain cradles and repaired farm implements. He may have carved and chiseled the intricate trimwork in the house next door.

Sebastian died, and in 1952 his son Charles passed away. Miss Shoup, Charles's spinster daughter, boarded up the workshop and remained in the house into her nineties. At least two of her cats stayed around, loitering outside the house or squeezing into the dilapidated woodshop. After all, it was home.

The historic house and shop had intrigued Cyndy Winfield since she was a girl. But not until she considered purchasing the properties did she learn the building was a woodshop. It was serendipitous. Her retired husband, Ron, is a carpenter, and both are cat lovers.

The Winfields bought the properties and replaced the rotting floors, fixed the sagging roof, and shored up the crumbling foundation. "It was a money pit," said Cyndy. It was also wintertime.

"The snow was blowing when we noticed a brown-striped tiger cat that just wouldn't go away," said Cyndy. "As we painted indoors, we watched her through frosted windows." Cyndy and Ron watched her meow beseechingly from the top of the big tire on Ron's truck, *please, let me in.*

How can you resist a cat that has a mouth shaped like a perpetual smile? Cyndy started feeding her. Later, she learned from the gentleman next door that Miss Shoup had originally owned fifteen cats. Herman said the whereabouts of most were unknown.

From the first invitation indoors, the grinning cat they named Cheesecake acted as if it was her birthright to be in the house. As Cyndy recalled, "When we let her in, she didn't respond like most cats entering an unfamiliar place. She pranced around, as if noticeably aware of what was what. She jumped on the window seat and went to sleep, at home again.

"She likes the back porch, too. It's nice and sunny with its windows on three sides. She curls up on any available chair out there," said Cyndy.

A month later, a black cat came seeking an invitation to dinner. Both she and the stout-legged Cheesecake belonged to Miss Shoup's brood. Before

the Winfields had arrived, Herman occasionally fed the famished pair. Hungry beggars though they had become, near the Shoup house they were at home.

In a divided half of the old workshop, Ron strips varnish, repairs unsteady chair legs, and builds custom pieces for friends, in the company of Cricket, the black cat. She goes next door to the house only when customers are gone. She sleeps on Ron's lap in the woodshop or in her basket on the workbench, or on the cat tree Ron built by nailing platforms between branches.

Cheesecake prefers the antique store in the house where Cyndy sells collectibles of glassware, furniture, jewelry, and popular midcentury modern pieces like blond Heywood-Wakefield furniture.

"Cheesecake has a following among the clientele," said Cyndy. "She's the counter cat. Unlike

Cricket, Cheesecake prefers any place where people will pet her."

Cheesecake and Cricket visit Herman every day, taking the little path leading through the broken fence. Since Herman's wife died, he depends on their daily visits even more. However, he still calls them Blackie and Tiger, the names he had chosen when he used to feed them.

In the eye of each beholder, only one place is home. For the cats and the Shoups, there was no place like the Coloma house and woodshop.

Cyndy's mother says Miss Shoup would be happy with what has transpired on her properties, and that two of her cats are at home. "Ron and I feel that way, too. Nothing will happen to the old place during our watch," Cyndy promised. "It's home away from home for us and will always be home to Cricket and Cheesecake."

Home is more than a house. It's where we listen to crickets as we fall asleep and make cheesecake at Thanksgiving. It's family and laughter and games. It's the driveway where we played hopscotch, and the knothole on the wooden steps where we stubbed our toes. It's the sidewalk where we rode our tricycle, and the curb where we parked and kissed. It's Christmastime, when Auntie played the piano and everyone sang carols. It's also a refuge for cats—the place where they are happiest and at rest.

Given all the pleasantries of life, the soul is still homeless if it's not *at home* with God. The heart longs for more than shelter. It yearns for the hearth of God's love and the welcome mat of forgiveness. There's no place like home and none other like God.

The Tail End:

Walt Disney's hit film, *Homeward Bound: The Incredible Journey*, is a family classic about two dogs and a cat that travel across mountains and plains on their way home to find their owners. The cat amid the dogs makes the threesome of pets a winsome trio.

Cyndy sells real estate, runs the antique business on weekends, and cares for ten cats at home. Six were rescued from a gas station; she *intended* to place them but hasn't! Least of all, Bette Davis, the big-eyed cat named after the actress. Ron enjoys carpentry in his vintage woodshop, and his good pal Cricket.

The Rhythm of Balance

The sleep of a laborer is sweet.

—Ecclesiastes 5:12 NIV

PURR-rayer:

Dear God, may I heed the needs of my body while I toil for the necessities of life.

At South Regal Lumber Yard, there's a lot of lifting, loading, and hauling. There's plenty of muscle and sweat, and a twelve-pound calico cat named Toes who oversees all the action.

Named after the extra digits on each front paw—seven by count—Toes first arrived with two feral cats that were captured in a humane trap at the lumberyard. Wild cats like these regularly hunted rodents and multiplied in the acreage behind the property. To keep their numbers manageable, the lumberyard allowed a farmer to take the trapped cats away from the hazards of busy arterials. He then gave them a country home in his barn, feeding them in exchange for their mice-hunting skills. The barn should have been Toes's destination, but she had other ideas.

In the jumble of three cats, scrambling in the trap to avoid the hands of a couple of lumbermen, two cats escaped. Toes also jumped out but didn't flee. She sat down beside the cage and looked at her captors as if to say, *What was all that about?*

Grateful to be free from the frenzy inside the cage, she moseyed toward the lumberyard employees, rubbed their booted ankles, and decided to stay.

Lawrence the clerk has fed Toes for two years. "We're a dump site for unwanted cats," he explained. "I've seen people throw cats over our cyclone fence. The cats stay because the back field is a source of food."

Toes slowly encroached on all the buildings and the storefront. Not yet a year old, she was "in the family way" soon after she came. With little promotion from the employees, her six kittens landed good homes with customers.

Toes must like the smell of wood, the sound of whirring saws, and the hum of a forklift. She especially likes Harry's red Dodge pickup. She rolls and suns herself in the truck bed and naps on the roof of the cab.

She hangs out on lumber stacks in the warehouse, passes customers in the store aisles, and pads through sawdust in the workshop. "She's always around—in a bin full of nails or in her favorite sleeping spot on the duct-tape display," said Lawrence. If she wants attention, she swats at passersby. Most people ignore her, but some pet her as they walk by.

She likes the mostly male employees and tolerates children of customers—if she's in a good mood. Lumberyard co-owner Scott Case said Toes hates the dogs that sometimes accompany contractors and remodelers into the store. "She chases 'em off!" he tattled.

Like pencils and a notepad, Toes is an everyday item on the store countertop. If she's asleep, the clerks shelve the tape measure or calculator on her gray, tan, and peach-patched fur. She lies motionless, blocking the view of the computer screen, which is housed under the glass counter. Attempting an inventory search is an awkward task with a cat in the way. But a

Kitty Wit:
Insomnia is never an issue for a cat.

gentle shove moves Toes aside. If she's miffed by the interference, she bats the stapler onto the floor.

Like a weight-conscious woman, she's often on the hardware scale; her tail usually covers the digital readout. She stays put until removed by a clerk who needs to weigh a bag of screws.

"You never know where you'll see her," said Lawrence. "We lift the tarp off a unit of lumber, and there's Toes." Employees usually cross paths with her several times a day.

While South Regal Lumber benefits from their mouse X-Terminator, there's one disadvantage to her services. She totes her vermin trophies to the counter near the front door, hoping for applause.

Toes corners mice or sleeps unless she's feigning herself as the cat burglar. One morning at about 3:30

a.m., the alarm system alerted Scott to trouble at the yard. "It rings at my house and at John's," he said. "We go check out the property and the doors, and then look in the store."

Scott puts Toes in the warehouse when he leaves at night. Otherwise, her movements trigger the security beams in the storefront. "That night, I *knew* I'd put her out." She sleeps in the warehouse but gets in the store if she's determined.

"If she's not in the store," he said, "I check the keypad to see what zones are set off." Suspicion was high. "Two areas were activated, which was different from normal.

"When we flipped on the store lights, we saw an eight-foot area of broken ceiling, and Toes was walking around the store. She'd squeezed between the first and second levels of the store and fallen through the false ceiling."

Bleary-eyed but relieved, John and Scott reset the alarm. They were glad the fright was only Toes, likely in pursuit of a mouse. Then again, she may have broken in just to sleep in her cushy foam bed on the duct-tape display.

Few people balance work and rest as Toes balances mouse hunts and catnaps. Much of society scorns idleness and acclaims labor. But poised between occupation and sleep is a posture of balance. Stay on your Toes and work hard, but know when to tuck them in and snooze for a while.

 The Tail End:

Without sleep, you can't dream; without work, you can't fulfill your dreams.

Clifford Case founded South Regal Lumber, in Spokane, Washington, in 1949. The family-owned business is now operated by Harry, John, and Scott Case.

Contagious Peace

And the God of peace will be with you.

—Philippians 4:9 NIV

PURR-rayer:

Dear God, help me cling to you for tranquility during the agonizing and inexplicable events of life, so I have peace to share with others.

Tall and classy Robi Railey shares her century-old office with two cats named after icons from literature—"Romeo" of romantic lore, and "The Princess" of fairy tales. Everybody loves Romeo, the ample brown tabby, and everyone says The Princess, a long-haired calico, is the fairest of them all. But for Robi, her grandson, Zackary Camarda, is a true story hero.

Robi's Allstate business is located in the old Pine Creek Dairy Creamery, a 1908 building listed on the Historic Register in Spokane, Washington. "When I was shopping for a building, Zackary was diagnosed a second time with neuroblastoma cancer." Understating her emotions, she said, "It was a hard day."

Before buying the two-story brick structure, she knew she wanted a cat at her work site; but now, she *needed* a cat. Robi's kitty at home was aging, so she turned to the pound for an office cat.

"I'm a cat fanatic," said Robi. "Cats make me calm and happy." As a child, she spent summers on a farm in Iowa with her grandmother. "The first thing I did when I arrived was kick off my shoes, run to the barn, and search the haystacks for newborn kittens."

Robi turned to Romeo for comfort during her grandson's ordeal. Zackary's first diagnosis, at age three and one half, led to surgery, chemotherapy, and other recommended treatments. Six months after celebrating one year of remission, the villain cells returned. "We knew it was a death sentence." Robi sighed and looked away. "No one had ever survived it twice," she said.

Shouldering both her daughter's pain and her own, Robi drove to the pound to look for a cat. She and a tabby locked eyes. She lifted him from the cage and sat down. "He'd already selected me, and I knew it. After circling three times in my lap, he lay down." Instantly lovesick, Robi and the male tabby left the pound together.

When her girlfriend dropped in at the office, the cat was still unnamed. She noticed how the clients admired him. "Everybody *loves* him, Robi! Name him Romeo." Allstate patrons can pay premiums online or by phone, but some pay in person, just for a calf rub from Romeo and a look at his handsome, broad face.

During the months when Zackary's health declined, Romeo helped Robi face her workload. "Following my visits to the hospital to see Zacky, if Romeo hadn't been at the office, I couldn't have phoned clients nor done paperwork. I was losing my firstborn grandchild. When I'd pick up Romeo, the stress would lessen and I'd feel okay—at least enough to function." Soon after, Robi's therapeutic cat had a similar, calming effect upon a feline acquaintance named The Princess.

> Kitty Wit:
> Essentials for cat owners:
> food, litter, and a lifetime supply of lint rollers

Throughout the two years before little Zacky's passing, Romeo thrived as the sole cat at the office until Robi took in The Princess. The first few days, Romeo sensed The Princess's fear of her new surroundings. He tagged behind her, seemingly fretful about her uneasiness. But Romeo's gentle attention smoothed her transition. The temporary boarder became a purr-manent resident, and The Princess and Romeo have bonded like epoxy.

The pair of cats lounges on a wicker chair and on a wide windowsill facing a busy arterial. A double door keeps them safely inside the entrance. From the sidewalk, frequent onlookers worry about Romeo and The Princess if the cats aren't visible in the window.

A few homeless people, from the House of Charity, drop in and pet them.

When children accompany parents, Robi hears their enthusiasm as they tromp upstairs to the lobby, and ask, "Will we get to see the kitties?"

Besides Robi's insurance patrons, customers from the adjacent hair salon who access from Robi's office, also benefit from the cats' friendliness. Romeo and The Princess like to visit the salon. Surprisingly, they're not put off by the pungent odors of wave solution. They nap on the warm laps of the salon's regulars.

Romeo and The Princess are okay with their office residence and lifestyle, with their twosome companionship, and their doting owner.

Despite her grandson's passing, Robi, also, is at peace. "Zacky was only eight when he died," she said. "He had his purpose for being here. I'm really okay with it, and Zacky's okay."

Roughly six months before he died, Robi and Zacky sat at a restaurant over lunch. Zacky laid down the crayon he held, folded his arms, and leaned forward.

"So, Gramma," he asked, "are you gonna be okay?"

"I paused and then nodded," said Robi. "'Yes, Zacky. I'm going to be okay. I am,'" she emphasized. It was a certain but hard-won peace for a grandmother, passed to her from her grandson.

The "okay" of peace is an infectious state of heart. Mutual strength is shared in the two-way reassurance that someone we love is at peace. Accepting tragedy often begins with the consolation that the person of our concern is okay. It was the concern of even Romeo when The Princess first arrived. Caring about the peace of others is the way of God, the way of Romeo, and the exemplary way of a grandmother.

 The Tail End:

A "tabby cat" is not a breed of cat, but a color pattern of stripes or whorls or even spots. If you prefer a specific breed, keep this in mind: 20 percent of shelter cats are purebreds.

Robi Railey has owned and managed her Allstate agency for thirty years. She is the mother of three daughters and three surviving grandchildren and enjoys investing, traveling, and golfing.

Encounters with Mystery

Beyond all question,

the mystery of godliness is great.

—1 Timothy 3:16 NIV

PURR-rayer:

Dear God, I am grateful that one day You will explain all the unknowns.

One winter evening, Ronna Snyder noticed the flicker of a large gold kitten skittering across the frosty deck of her Idaho ranch house. Even she, the ardent cat hater, could not ignore a half-grown cat eking out a living in a landscape of snow, devoid of sustenance—save a mouse or two.

She warmed milk and called to the feral cat, who stared at her as it would a stalking coyote before disappearing under moonlight. Ronna left the milk on the deck. The next morning the bowl was dry, and there was no sign of the furry gold mystery. The cycle repeated night after night as Ronna obliged the stealthy cat.

A couple of weeks later she noticed the movement of the same amber head under the deck. With more obligation than enthusiasm she called, "Here kitty, kitty!" Thankless and lionlike, the cat hissed and spit, exposing its incisors like its saber-toothed ancestor.

"Blasted cat!" Ronna murmured. Regardless, she provided the meal like a servile wife waiting on a demanding husband.

After retreating to the house, she secretly watched the hungry visitor skulk from the shadows, eyes darting and ears cocked for the sound of the doorknob—a sound that now signaled an offering of food for the waif of a cat.

The sequence grew regular. The cat appeared, inspected the deck for handouts, met Ronna's gaze through the window, and gobbled the proffered meal.

In the Snyders' critter-littered farmland, where animals are a renewable resource among predators, the cagey kitten had survived the population of owls and coyotes. As Ronna pondered the cat's prowess, she wondered with amazement, *Am I actually admiring the kitten's chutzpah?*

Ronna fretted to her cat-lover friend, "What if it's a female and I get overrun by equally wild-eyed offspring?"

"Relax," said Niki, "it's likely a male." She explained that calicos are largely females and yellow tabbies are more often males.

Ronna lightened up, but only a little, and continued responding to the nightly bidding of the illusive intruder she now called Mystery. The obvious fattening of the cat's once bony rib cage and prominent hip bones fueled Ronna's feeding routine. One concession made by the cat also encouraged Ronna; the kitten no longer postured and spit at her.

Several weeks into the cat's still-rude distancing, Ronna decided she was done with the one-sided relationship. She sat near the food bowl and refused to leave. Wrapped in a bathrobe, Ronna waited in the bitter cold. Mystery had two choices. To longingly observe the tempting meal and abstain until Ronna went back inside, or to do something beyond the cat's wild nature—trust her.

Both of them in a standoff, Mystery looked on, crouched like a cougar and growling in a throaty rumble. At last, hunger overcame fear as Mystery hunkered toward the food, only three feet away from Ronna.

Kitty Wit:
Cats are like celebrities;
they love to make a dramatic entrance.

In hushed tones, she coaxed Mystery closer to the bowl. Ronna made cooing noises like baby talk, the common prattle of cat lovers.

"I've simply lost my flippin' mind," Ronna said to herself. "What attracts me to this cat?" When she glanced behind at her husband, who watched through the window, she read his expression. He, too, was bemused by her inexplicable infatuation with Mystery.

By then the nightly meetings were a ritual. Ronna spoke the lingo of "coo-coo-kitty," with Mystery cautiously moving closer as Ronna pulled the bowl nearer to herself each time.

Within a week the snarling and tentative Mystery let Ronna touch the golden fur with her fingertips. And eventually the cat's guttural threats softened and even gave way to an occasional and ingratiating purr.

Despite their progress, Mystery's tense body language gave warning: *Don't push it, and don't even think about handling me.* Once before, Ronna had breached that boundary without success.

Ronna's ignorance of things feline mandated another call to her author-friend, who writes cat books. "What is it with this cat's dough-kneading paw dance?" she asked.

"He loves you!" Niki exclaimed.

By then Ronna could stroke the still cautious Mystery from head to tail tip. Ronna liked it, though she suspected, and even feared, she might turn into a "crazy cat lady."

Having bridged the chasm between herself and Mystery, she felt a warm sense of accomplishment. She had won the trust of an animal whose very survival motivated its fear. And besides, Ronna realized that she was as mysterious to Mystery as the cat's feline ways were to her. "My relationship with Mystery is no different from any human relationship," she said. "They begin with trust and a respect for boundaries. And even at best, every relationship involves a bit of the unknown."

Life is filled with mysteries impossible to decipher. Like Ronna, we enter relationships we might not have chosen. We bridge chasms of understanding as broad as those between animal and humankind. We may even experience a mysterious change of heart like Ronna's compassion toward a starving cat. How does it happen?

The greatest mystery of all is God Himself. If we could comprehend Him, He would be too small for the title of God. For to encounter mystery is to encounter the God who knows more than we, and to accept His mysteries lessens the demand to solve them.

The Tail End:

"Red" is the professional term for the color of a cat's coat, more often described as gold, orange, or ginger. The gene for the red color is sex linked. For that reason, red cats are usually males.

Adapted from the original story by award-winning writer Ronna Snyder, author of *Hot Flashes from Heaven: When Midlife and Menopause Meet*. Ronna is also a speaker and photographer who can be contacted at http://www.ronnasnyder.com.

Ins-purr-ation

The Spirit of God has made me; the breath of the Almighty gives me life.

—Job 33:4 NIV

PURR-rayer:

Dear God, breathe on me.

The straightforward words in the newspaper ad withheld no facts from the prospective reader. "Blue-eyed white deaf cat."

Speaking aloud to neither husband nor friend, Jackie Brauer addressed only herself. "I don't want a deaf cat." For starters, *why have a cat who'll never hear the sound of its name or the familiar voice of its owner?* she reasoned. Avowing her preference, she stated again. "I don't want a deaf cat."

For weeks Jackie had rattled the pages of the Cats for Sale columns. In her hunt to adopt, she whizzed past countless depictions of available cats—like Fluffkins, "a sweet lap cat," and Spencer, who preferred a "childless home," said the owners. Another was Stripes, a red tabby, who was billed as nice, neutered, though "sometimes nefarious." The truth was told.

Jackie felt no attraction to Fluffkins, Spencer, or Stripes, with or without their owners' embellishments. But the words "blue-eyed white deaf cat" swept across her heart, seemingly intent on delivering a message: "That's *your* cat."

After thirty minutes of exchanges with herself—"Yes, no, no, yes,"—Jackie called the listed number.

"I wish you'd called earlier," said the lady hosting the stray. "Some college students just took her. If it doesn't work out, I'll call you back." Despite Jackie's initial ambivalence, she sighed with disappointment.

A month later she was still reading the pet ads as regularly as steeping her morning tea. The routine search continued in many editions of the *Spokesman-Review* until she saw a phrase she least expected. "Blue-eyed white deaf cat." The evocative words beckoned her as convincingly as at first.

Compelled and curious, Jackie tapped the seven numbers on the telephone keypad and heard the same caring voice. "Oh! I'm so glad you called. I lost your number! Things didn't work out for the students. One needs back surgery and the others have no time for the cat."

Though not wishing the agony of surgery on anyone, Jackie was suddenly elated to learn the cat would be hers.

Hours later she met the blue-eyed beauty who lived in a world of silence. One look at her tanzanite eyes and wavy white fur, and Jackie bonded with the cat.

But how do you communicate with a hearing-impaired pet? The big question waited while Jackie's granddaughter loved on the cat and came up with a name without even trying.

When three-year-old Chloe held "Gramma's kitty," she pressed her nose in the fur and said, "Gramma, this cat smells!" Jackie noted that Chloe did not say, "This cat stinks!"

The undefined smell did not stop Chloe from caressing the newcomer. Every time she nestled her face in the soft coat, she declared, "This cat smells."

At suppertime Jackie lifted the cat into Chloe's arms for another hug. "Gramma!" she announced. "This cat smells . . . like vanilla!"

Jackie took a whiff from the thick fur and smelled the trace of fragrance. "She does, Chloe! Let's *name* her Vanilla."

Was the scent from a candle? Or a lotion from the hands of the girl who transported the cat? No mistake, the scent was sweet vanilla, the very essence of Jackie's new companion.

Christening Vanilla was still no solution to

> ### Kitty Wit:
> Cats and women are alike. You can spend a lifetime with them and still be mystified.

communication. How would Jackie summon her for kitty vittles or alert her when necessary? Some suggested thumping; others said to wave her arms or even stomp. But Jackie insisted on a method of a kindlier sort. "I just won't stomp at my cat," she said.

So she asked Denny, a close family friend, who replied instantly. "Just blow on her!"

The idea was a natural. The movement of a cat's hair is a God-given sensor. A puff of Jackie's warm breath would be little different than a mild summer breeze.

Sure enough, Vanilla responded without alarm. A mere wisp of air was enough to stir her. "If she was asleep," said Jackie, "she'd lift her head and meow as if to say, *Yes?*" Jackie and Vanilla were talking!

With time, they developed their own cat-speak.

"When Vanilla is across the room, I use the common signal for 'come,' by flexing my fingers on my upturned palm." Since Jackie must be physically close to Vanilla to converse, either by a breath of air or a hand sign, Vanilla's hearing loss fosters togetherness. Consequently, Jackie views Vanilla's so-called impairment as an enhancement, not a disability.

When the vacuum roars, the doorbell rings, or Jackie's granddaughter squeals, Vanilla is tranquil in her private environment of quiet. Indifferent to cat toys, Vanilla plays on the carpet with imaginary bugs by stalking, pouncing, and rolling her long tresses on the pretend prey.

In spite of hearing loss, Vanilla has acute sensory perception. She even recognizes if Jackie, a diabetic, is having health problems. On two separate occasions she awoke Jackie in the night when her blood sugar fell dangerously low. Since Vanilla doesn't hear Jackie if she leaves the house, Vanilla scolds her with staccato meows when she returns.

Jackie has discovered how hearing is perceived through other means than the ears. Like God who breathed life into his creation and changed a shape of clay into a companion, Jackie's first breath upon Vanilla began a relationship of communication and love.

Though sometimes impaired at hearing God's voice, we more easily recognize the soft breath of His presence in the help of a friend, a phone call with good news, or a casserole from a neighbor when we're ill. If we are desperately longing for God's audible response, we can be watchful and grateful for those silent signs of His presence.

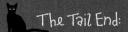

The Tail End:

In British Sign Language the sign for CAT is a quick movement of splayed fingers outward from the cheeks. In American Sign Language, the sign is first fingers and thumbs rubbing imaginary whiskers.

Jackie Brauer served as an air force medical corpsman, a switchboard operator, and a crowd manager at entertainment facilities. A mother of two adult daughters, she enjoys Bible study, gardening, and babysitting Chloe.

Not About a Cat

For God so loved the world that He gave His one and only Son, that whoever believes in Him shall not perish but have eternal life.

—John 3:16 NIV

PURR-rayer:

Dear God, as I grapple with loss, let me hear the message in my temporary privations.

On a winter night in Bowie, Maryland, Lynn Baldwin mistook the noise of an opossum for her deceased father's missing cat, which had disappeared under her guardianship. Eighteen days before, Lloyd Sloger had succumbed to a diseased heart. Grieving the loss of her father and failing to fulfill his last wish for Calico, Lynn felt heartsick. She couldn't bring back her father, but she had to find his cat. Once again, she prayed the request she had repeated countless times. "Dear Lord Jesus, please send home my dad's cat."

For five years the calico cat had lived with Lloyd, a full-time mechanic and part-time caregiver. A devoted Christian, Lloyd was frequently off to a pharmacy or supermarket for someone. He cooked for others and taxied many to clinics. He looked after his blind brother, nursed Lynn's chronically ill mother, and never neglected the needs of his own mother or a widowed mother-in-law.

By the time he was eighty, his children lived far away and other family members had died, so he turned his attention to cats.

Though Lloyd lived in Ohio, his daughter talked with him almost every day. Lynn would call and inquire, "How are you today, Dad, and how is Ms. Calico?" Lynn and her husband drove three hundred miles every six weeks to check on him. She and her dad baked apple pies and intermittently addressed the cat. "Thank you, Calico, for being such a beautiful cat," Lloyd would say to his kitty. Calico scampered after him by day. At night the ding of a kitchen timer signaled bedtime, and Calico would run to Lloyd's room.

When Lloyd was eighty-six, his cardiologist informed him that a shadow of cancer on his lung disqualified him from the list of candidates waiting for a heart valve. He declined chemotherapy and accepted the prognosis of only months to live.

"I cried the whole week of my visit," said Lynn. "But Dad said it was time for him to begin eternal life."

"My time is in the hands of Jesus, Lynn, and I have no fear." Lloyd mentioned only one concern. "I just want to know what will happen to Calico."

Lynn assured him Calico would remain with the family. "Bravely, I returned to Maryland," said Lynn, "promising Dad I'd be back in ten days. But eight days later he went to be with his Lord."

After the memorial service Lynn wandered through his house feeling cheated of seeing him one last time. She curled up with Calico and wept.

The next day the Baldwins drove to Maryland with Calico in a cardboard carrier on the backseat of their car. She was so scared that she chewed a hole in the box. "So I took her from the carrier," said Lynn, "and held her on my lap. Still, she shivered with fear. After pulling into our driveway, I stepped from the car while clasping Calico tightly. The shrill bark of a neighboring dog sent Calico flying from my grip with the strength of a tiger.

> Kitty Wit:
> If cats are in a hurry,
> it's for their own agenda, never yours.

Our hearts in a panic, we tracked her through pine trees, shrubbery, and thickets, but she bounded from sight. We canvassed the area, posted signs, consulted shelters, and phoned veterinarians." Authorities offered little encouragement. The pampered cat had never been outdoors, never caught a mouse, never been cold, dehydrated, or half starved.

Lynn folded her dad's shirt in a box on the porch, set a live trap, and left food along the perimeters of the house. For each of the next fourteen nights a raccoon or a possum entered the cage.

Daily, Lynn continued her petition. "Dear Lord Jesus, please send home my dad's cat." And every night she stood on the porch and called Calico's name into the chilly December air.

"My heart was broken. I couldn't fulfill Dad's wish for Calico, much less even find her," she said. "Constantly, I thought of Dad. As if talking to him, I'd say, 'I'm sorry, Dad. I wish I could talk to you. I didn't get to see you as I'd planned. What will I do without you, Dad? Where are you? I need you!'"

On day fifteen she heard a rustle on the porch as she set out Christmas decorations, and she prayed again, "Dear Lord Jesus, please send home my dad's cat." Ever so slowly, she opened the door and peered out. To her dismay, she saw a possum eating the cat food and upsetting the bowl. Her hopes spilled like the kitty's milk. Calico could be miles away, perhaps too scared to approach anyone, and maybe not even alive.

Lynn picked up the small figure of baby Jesus from the crèche on the table, and rephrased her prayer. Slightly indignant, she said, "Dear Lord Jesus, please ask my dad just how important that cat is to him!"

With hands on hips, she stared at the Christmas decorations, trying to focus on the task at hand. But, amazingly, her prayer was being answered right then. "Only ten minutes later I heard a meow and peeked again. A mix of disbelief and elation filled my heart as Calico walked indoors," Lynn exclaimed.

The story of Calico is not about a cat, says Lynn, and not even about her earthly father. It's about the heavenly Father, whom Lynn pictures turning to her dad and saying, "Lloyd, Lynn needs assurance that you're with Me. Let's guide Calico home."

To encourage belief in the wonder of everlasting life, God sometimes gives a sign by returning a calico cat.

The Tail End:

A pet is legally defined as property. Your last will and testament may include the appointment of a consenting person or organization to adopt your cat and allocate funds for its care.

Lynn Baldwin is the child care coordinator for the Maryland-National Capital Park and Planning Commission, an adjunct professor at Prince George's Community College, and an appointed official on the Prince George's County Commission for Women.

Particular Person Meets Purr-ticular Cat

I praise you because

I am fearfully and wonderfully made.

—Psalm 139:14 NIV

PURR-rayer:

Dear God, I praise you for your intimate knowledge of me, so lovingly evident in your gifts.

I'd sure have a cat if she was just like Mitzi. Kathi remembers her thought and how she dismissed the wish as quickly as it tiptoed through her head. No cat she had ever noticed was like her sister's cat, the well-behaved Mitzi.

The petite and prissy kitty appealed to Kathi, herself a feminine and proper lady. Polite Mitzi even asked permission before jumping on a lap. A gentle stretch of her calico leg and a paw tap on the knee formed her request. She didn't jump on tabletops, nibble on plants, clamber up draperies, or dismantle the Christmas tree—Santa forbid!

Sadly, during Kathi's occasional musings about Mitzi, her life collapsed in a series of unrelated, agonizing downturns. Within seven months her youngest son moved out, her banking career ended, and her double-decade marriage dissolved.

But an improvement of events arrived in the form of a cat. Kathi's sister, who had moved to Saudi Arabia, left Mitzi with Kathi. Together, cat and divorcée grew deep in their affection. While riding the tide of her emotions and rebuilding her life, Kathi found constant consolation in her feline helpmate. "For example," said Kathi, "to ease my hurt, I'd turn on music. It became Mitzi's clue to offer me cuddle-comfort."

For the next 11 years, the perfect cat shared the vagaries of life with Kathi and her later husband, Ron.

"When Mitzi died of complications from an injury, I was amazed at the trauma," she said. "But after a period of mourning, I decided I *could* live without a cat." Dominating her conclusion was the implausibility of finding another prim kitty precisely suited to her lifestyle, preferences, and emotions. Kathi was particular.

So she prayed. God, I'm so spoiled by Mitzi. And what if I select a cat I dislike? I guess if you want me to have another, you'll pretty much have to bring it to the back door.

"Eighteen months later, I heard rumors about a kitten hanging around the church where I serve as women's pastor," she said. The worship minister spent a fair amount of time at his desk with the cat. Outdoors, a toweled box with lid and cutout door

provided boarding for the black-and-white kitten. DeeAnn, the director of children's ministry, was mediating for the homeless kitten, hoping it might fill a role as official church cat.

On the opposing side of the debate, Gary, the grounds supervisor, grew tired of the cat's thankless offerings, here-a-little and there-a-lot, on the property. Cats aren't typically the cause for church splits, but as the story jokingly hints, this innocent feline created some hostility among the staff.

One afternoon Gary grabbed the furry intruder. Destined for the pound, the God-sent cat was "saved

Kitty Wit:
Definition of a cat scan: the disdainful glance [of a] cat when her demands are not promptly met

by grace" right there on the lawns of the church. She scrambled free from Gary's arms and never went near him again. So Gary set a deadline for all cat lovers on staff. "Find a home for her or she *will* go elsewhere."

At this stage in the dispute, Kathi heard about the cat and the scrimmage. The church's cat sympathizers coaxed Kathi, pleaded, and finally resorted to pressure. "It's time you had a new cat, and this one needs a home—quick."

"They all but dragged me outdoors," said Kathi, "just to take a look at her." The bitter temperatures of November and impending snowfall added to the force of a decision.

"Weakening, I talked to my husband. I also interviewed Paul, the staffer who'd been lap-sitting

'I'm not even a cat lover,' he admitted, 'but this cat is special.'"

By now Kathi had almost forgotten her prayer after Mitzi's passing, when she overheard a discussion in the church office that widened her eyes.

One person informed the other. "You've heard, haven't you? The cat pretty much just showed up at the back door."

"My brain sucked a mental breath," said Kathi. "I remembered the words of my prayer. Was this the back door cat that God had chosen for me?"

Not fully trusting, Kathi outlined a list of contingencies sure to quell an agreement that she adopt the cat—*unless* God had indeed brought *this* cat to *this* back door.

All conditions were readily met and Zoe went to her first real home. The dainty kitten, marked by a triangular white blaze over her left eye, soon proved her worthiness as a fastidious, intelligent, and respectful cat—"just like Mitzi." When Zoe strolls to the bedroom each morning, she refrains from even the temptation of Kathi's luxurious mattress. She takes to her leopard-print kitty bed instead.

"Zoe was God's choice in every particular," said Kathi. "And He pretty much delivered her to my back door."

Cats are finicky but so are their owners. Yet a personal God can connect a particular person to a purr-ticular cat. God knows what foods we savor, what color we favor, and what cat we will love. He designed our desires, requirements, and preferences. He is well acquainted with all our particulars.

The Tail End:

One of the oldest representations of a pet cat is a figurine found in Hacilar, a Neolithic site in Turkey. The statuette, dated at more than seven-thousand years old, shows a woman cuddling a cat.

Kathi Jingling serves as women's pastor at a Life Center Foursquare Church in Spokane, Washington. In her free time she haunts thrift stores, entertains often, and loves to snuggle with her new grandson. She and her husband enjoy reading, kayaking, biking, traveling, and times spent with their adult children.

The Divine Drama

*Many are the plans in a man's heart,
but it is the Lord's purpose that prevails.*

—Proverbs 19:21 NIV

PURR-rayer:
Dear God, whether minor role or major, I will value my part in the divine plot.

Aspiring actors and homeless cats are alike. They're waiting to be discovered.

With two golden eyes fixed on theater life, a lost cat began making appearances between the shed and a side entrance at The Rocky Hock Playhouse. Each year five Broadway-style musicals draw thousands of visitors to the Christian theater in Edenton, North Carolina.

The cat was a wanna-be actor, or so he thought. Having eliminated the sparse mouse population on the theater property, he had become a *starving* wanna-be actor.

In February 2002, the Playhouse hosted a dinner in conjunction with their Valentine production. Following a matinee, Jeff Emmerich, co-owner and director, with his wife Gloria, noticed the tame though cautious cat performing outdoors for the departing audience.

In his everyday costume of black stripes on gray, he dropped to the ground in dramatic fashion. He rolled left and right, stretching his underside to display a downy yellow tummy and a tawny undercoat. The stray cat even rehearsed his best line. "Me-ooow!" Perhaps the whole act was an attempt at an unscheduled audition.

After a few days he was earning his supper as a showstopper. Jeff and Gloria, suspecting he was abandoned, tossed banquet leftovers of baked fish and roast beef to the hungry cat. "After a week or so, he let us pick him up," said Jeff. In honor of the cat's sideshow theatrics, Jeff named him Thespis, after the first male actor in the history of Greek theater.

With no roles for a feline, the Emmerichs ignored Thespis's bid for the stage and took him home. Thespis's youthful good looks and natural talent for stealing the show won him the purr-manent role of house cat in the Emmerich family. They hired him in exchange for his room, board, and a lifetime of love.

Being discovered was the big break of Thespis's first year of life. But after a few weeks in the Emmerich home, he made a discovery of his own. He preferred residential life and an occasional outdoor foray better than theater. At home, he was center stage all the time.

Only once did he reconsider acting. When Gloria wrote the production *Paul, Fearless Lion of God,* Thespis felt especially suited for the part. After all, he had grown to a bigger-than-average nineteen pounds. He swings a swelling number of ounces in his belly. Although Thespis might have looked the part of a lion,

the veterinarian had proposed a lean diet. So Gloria cast Jeff as the lionlike apostle for the play.

In the past six years Thespis has spent only five days in The Rocky Hock Playhouse. In 2003, when Hurricane Isabel slammed the eastern coastline with 110-mile winds, the Emmerichs and Thespis took shelter at the Playhouse, which is located ten miles from their wood-frame home. The move proved to be a wise choice as a safe haven. Isabel hurled a four-foot-long tree limb through the roof of their home. It hovered just above their daughter's pillow and on the same bed where Thespis slept regularly.

> ### Kitty Wit:
> If your wallet holds more pictures
> of your cats than of your kids,
> guess who gets more gifts at Christmas?

Thespis's best friend is also connected to the Playhouse. About three years after Thespis turned up, Jeff and Gloria began to consider a companion for him. On a drive to Virginia Beach, Jeff made a sudden stop for a closer look at a palm-size kitten crouched on the shoulder of the highway. He coaxed the black-and-white cat within reach of his grasp and carried him to the car. Gloria took one look and said, "We *must* name him Cluster!"

Besides writing the thirty musicals performed at The Rocky Hock Playhouse, Gloria sells homemade peanut clusters at all the shows. Her secret recipe a favorite of chocolate lovers, bears the label, "Mrs Cromley's Famous Peanut Clusters."

Kitten Cluster went home to meet Thespis, who

instantly infatuated Cluster. The kitten's affection was as irresistible to Thespis as Gloria's peanut clusters are to the Playhouse patrons.

Thespis continued as the leading man at home, and the talkative Cluster became the domestic director. The slender, long-haired tuxedo cat waves a full black tail, wears a white bib, and sports five-inch-long whiskers. Green eyes are set in a small roundish head. His cheeks are alternate colors, one black and one white, to match four white paws.

More wired than Thespis, Cluster initiates fierce wrestling matches with his companion. "Role-playing," says Jeff. "I suspect they're practicing for a sudden call to fill in for a scene of conflict at the Playhouse."

"They're hard fast friends," said Jeff. "They sleep together, and like Lipizzaner horses, they synchronize their steps as they prance through the house."

Though Thespis has lived close to the world of theater, he is happy at home without the noise of applause or the fawning attention of fans. Besides, he has Cluster as his sidekick.

Thespis had written a script for his life. Stage, mews-icals, and dance. But God changed his dreams of stardom to pleasant reality dramas on the set in the Emmerich home.

God the master playwright creates the libretto for each person's life. When we snatch the pen from God's fingers, we miss the music and the finale that He intends.

Follow God's score and don't reword the script. When the curtain falls, and you bow from this life, all heaven will applaud.

The Tail End:

Keep interested in your own career, however humble.

—Max Ehrmann
from his famous "Desiderata."

The Emmerichs founded The Rocky Hock Playhouse in 2000. Jeff, the artistic director, has directed over sixty major works and over thirty American productions. Gloria is the resident musical director, playwright, lyricist, composer, and arranger. In addition, the couple also entertains at venues abroad, and for American troops overseas. (Gloria's chocolates are sold to visitors at the theater and through their Web site, www.rockyhockplayhouse.com)

Wild Things

Forgive my hidden faults.

—Psalm 19:12 NIV

PURR-rayer:

Dear God, search my heart daily for inappropriate traveling companions.

After months of befriending a feral cat that Ronna Snyder named Mystery, one evening she noticed several silhouettes outside her Idaho ranch. Instead of one fur-coated Mystery, there were two, then three, and even a fourth mystery! But the most alarming of mysteries still lay ahead.

The sight of "three little kittens" flattened Ronna's hopes that her feline friend was a male. Having met her mister, Mystery was now parading three youngsters. "Instantly, I changed her name to Ms. Tery," said Ronna.

"My husband, Bill, and I would soon leave in the motor home for our annual trip south. I couldn't abandon the semiwild Ms. and her wilder kittens through the winter, so I told our caretaker, 'Feed the cats—*all* of them!'"

Ronna admitted she would miss the nightly bonding she had begun with Ms. Tery. "Though Ms. Tery was still guarded," said Ronna, "when I called, she ran to me purring. She let me lift her about six inches from the floor of our deck before she'd flex her claws and squirm loose." Relieved that Ms. Tery and her litter would be nourished, Ronna relaxed as the family left for the season on a snowy Christmas Day.

"With the mercury hovering at twenty degrees, we and three of our adult children headed first to Oregon. During an interlude at my daughter's home in Medford, I heard the faint mew of a cat and thought fondly of Ms. Tery. Distracted by the nostalgia, I grabbed a novel to offset my emotions.

"Our daughter and husband joined the family troupe, and we headed for Reno, climbing snow-laden passes to five-thousand-foot altitudes. To prevent the pipes from freezing and to lessen the 60-miles per hour wind chill, we switched on the RV's basement heater and forged on. Our sights were set on watching Reno's midnight extravaganza of fireworks on New Year's Eve.

"Bill and I stayed in the RV that first night in Reno and favored our energetic kids with the hotel suite. *We'll sleep better,* I reasoned." Not so. After an exhausting day and evening, Ronna heard the sound.

"In the center of the casino parking lot, at the heart of 'the city that never sleeps' was a noise louder than a slot machine hitting pay dirt," said Ronna.

"I screamed, 'Bill! Come here!' He raced through the front door, supposing the motor coach was in flames.

"'We have a stowaway!' I blurted.

"The piercing cry was the yowl of Ms. Tery, my golden momma-cat. I had a flashback to Medford and the cry I'd presumed belonged to a neighbor cat.

"Lodged in the gravel-coated undercarriage, Ms. Tery had survived the frigid, six-day, one-thousand-mile trip without food or water. Even less imaginable

was how I would catch the feral cat who'd never let me carry her." Ronna didn't worry long.

"Ms. Tery leapt from the wheel well, over the massive tires, and landed in my arms. I rushed the frantic cat into the warmth of the coach's interior while Bill and I stared in disbelief.

"It was three a.m. We had no cat food, no litter box! Wasn't this a vacation from cats? Like prophets foreseeing the doom, we surveyed the shiny leather couches in our beautiful motor coach and its gleaming kitchen cabinets. Our mind's eye envisioned claw-shredded leather and cherrywood shavings strewn on the cream-colored carpets."

Kitty Wit:
Cats are not inclined to admit their regrets

But Ronna ignored the gloomy prospects of feline vandalism. "I shifted my maternal gear into overdrive," she said. "I gave Ms. Tery some milk and canned tuna, and watched as she attacked it like a survivor among the fittest. Quickly satisfied, she paced between my legs in figure eights, and nudged my calves with affection. *How endearing,* I thought.

"I could finally admit that I truly adored that blasted little cat. I picked her up and nuzzled her cheek. Unlike the past, she snuggled and purred. I loved this little kitty who'd endured the odds of nature at our ranch, and an unfathomable journey beneath our RV.

"In hopes of some shut-eye, we put Ms. Tery in the shower stall, and her howling began. She had no more tolerance for confinement. So we buried our heads under pillows and prayed for sleep."

But Ronna couldn't wait until sunrise, she said. "I couldn't sleep, so I roused Bill and convinced him that Ms. Tery had needs *now*!

"Weary, but thankful for the navigation system in our towed car, we found a Wal-Mart where we purchased litter boxes, a carrier, and food, and formed plans for our kids to take her home on their return later that day.

"They promised to get Ms. Tery home safely, so we said good-bye to our brave little stowaway. Did I miss her? All trouble and bother?

"My first phone call home to the kids was to confirm Ms. Tery's arrival," Ronna admitted.

"Yeah, Mom," Ronna's son answered. "Ms. Tery didn't bail on us."

"And honey, are Ms. Tery's kittens eating from the feeder?" Ronna still worried.

"As we headed south to Phoenix, I gave Bill our son's positive report, and he replied in monotone, When we get home, maybe we'll make Ms. Tery a house cat.'"

Ronna looked through the window at the unbounded landscape of the Nevada desert, and smiled.

Stowaways aren't always four-footed, fur-coated, endearing creatures. Pride, resentment, and all manner of ill will, hidden in the soul, can ride on board until they finally surface like a half-wild cat leaping in our face.

Check your heart often. Don't journey through life with stowaways. Let God cleanse the heart of all "things wild."

 The Tail End:

Things concealed in the heart eventually emerge and reveal the contents of the soul.

Adapted from the original story by Ronna Snyder, author of *Hot Flashes from Heaven: When Midlife and Menopause Meet*. Ronna is also a speaker and photographer. Learn more about her at www.RonnaSnyder.com.

Danger at Bay

A friend
loves at all times.
—Proverbs 17:17 NIV

Dear God, when people bark at me, give me the backbone to hope for a friendship.

"Danger was a cool cat; some say a fool cat, a mean, lean, break-all-the-rules cat." So begins the rhyme by Libby Riddles, the first woman to win the Iditarod. Her storybook for children describes Danger, the tenacious cat she rescued from the Nome dog pound.

Danger had all it takes to live for fifteen years with fifty-seven sled dogs on the Alaskan frontier. He tried anything and usually succeeded at everything. His specialty was making friends by rebuffing intimidation.

Libby's illustrated book is a part-fiction tale about Danger and the dog team that led Libby to her first-place finish in the Iditarod

161

sled dog race. Though Danger was not actually a "lead cat," there's nothing fictional about the daring nature of Libby's real and intrepid feline or the fact of Libby's 1985 victory in the Iditarod.

When Libby adopted Danger, the six-month-old, gray-striped, short-haired stray with white chin, chest, and paws was in top form for Libby's bush-style existence. "I was really shook up after my previous cat died," said Libby. "So I went to the pound looking for a new cat that wasn't too young. The cat had to endure twenty to sixty degree subzero temperatures and life at an isolated cabin in Nelchina, northeast of Anchorage."

The indomitable cat exceeded Libby's expectations. He traveled with her by boat, car, and dogsled across the roughest icescapes in Alaska, as Libby prepared to race her team 1,150 miles from Anchorage to Nome.

"Danger wasn't fazed by anything from the day I got him," she said. For starters, he faced off with rude, growling dogs that didn't welcome a cat in their yard. Yet he won their trust. "You gotta have the right stuff to be the only cat in the dog yard," said Libby. "Sled dogs have no sense of humor."

"One of my testiest dogs was Bane. For certain, he was the bane of his litter. The other dogs were scared of him, and, of course, the cat and he ended up as best friends. When Danger stuck his nose in Bane's house, the dog didn't even move," Libby said.

But Danger had to learn his way around Libby's other tough huskies. Once he nearly got eaten by a couple of dogs for playing with one's tail.

When the yard dogs were pups, he bossed them around, and when they grew into adults, they still perceived Danger as someone bigger and in charge. He always proved he was no patsy. But he wasn't just tough; he spent a lot of time playing with them, too. He earned respect while making a friend.

In the fall Libby took Danger in a carrier on a fifty-mile sled-dog ride to a winter camp, where she fished for northern pike and whitefish. Few in the Eskimo village of Teller had ever seen a cat. They must've been surprised to observe Danger—whose only role models were dogs—tagging behind Libby to the post office every day.

Kitty Wit:
If you're limber enough to reach your toes with your tongue, you are probably a cat.

And imagine their awe when they saw the cat doing his own fishing if Libby ran out of moose meat for his dinner.

Libby had always loved cats. She grew up with five siblings in Minnesota along with family pets that included dogs, fish, and canaries. Pogo, a springer spaniel, was her shadow. "Although back then," Libby remarked, "I was much more of a cat person than a dog person, which is pretty funny when I ended up spending my life with forty to sixty dogs."

Libby's childhood dream of ranching and owning lots of animals led her up North instead of out West. A love for the icy frontier, and for her dogs, satisfied Libby long before someone suggested she run the Iditarod. But things changed the day she watched her first sled-dog race. "That part of me that loves nature began to sing," she said.

She didn't fool herself about the necessary endurance to participate. She raced a stretch of 180 miles before attempting the marathon. After long, arduous, freezing days of dog-mushing, Libby cuddled in a mummy bag with Danger, she said. "Up here, you use cats for heaters."

When Libby hosted sled-dog tours in the summertime, Danger lived with her in a tent on the shore of the Bering Sea. But he was no beach bum. "I finally had to put him on a leash in front of the tent," Libby said. "Otherwise, while I harnessed the dog team, he'd hop on the touring bus with a load of sightseers." That was Danger. Always making friends.

True to Libby's rhyme, Danger was a "cool cat." Cool enough to shake off the chill of the constant north wind.

Danger was a "fool cat." Fool enough to ignore the threats of the toughest dogs on the tundra.

Danger was a "mean cat." Mean enough to refuse intimidation for the sake of gaining a friend.

Danger was a "break-all-the-rules cat." Independent enough to convince every dog in the yard that he belonged there, and take the risks to make everyone happy in the end.

Like polar explorers who endangered their lives, Danger imperiled himself to make friends with the unfriendly. Initiating a relationship always involves risk, reluctance or even resistance from the would-be friend. But don't take offense. You'll gain many more friends by trying than if you flinched at a snarl and gave up your efforts.

The Tail End:

Cats who can get along with dogs are like people who are bilingual.
—Libby Riddles

Libby writes books, dog-wrangles for films, and lectures in Juneau for the Princess cruise line and at other venues. Her CD of many self-written tunes and the hardback and audio book, *Danger: The Dog Yard Cat*, are used in schools to help children learn to read. Her other books are *Storm Run* and *Race Across Alaska*. She lives in Homer, Alaska, with forty dogs and Maestro, her cat, who joined the household after Danger's passing. Learn more about Libby at www.libbyriddles.com

Ex-purr-t Guidance

The Lord will guide you always.

—Isaiah 58:11 NIV

PURR-rayer:

Dear God, forgive the arrogance that presumes humankind can succeed without your guidance.

Fortuitous for Jessica Bradshaw, the filmmakers for *National Geographic Explorer* planned to videotape a hunt for a lost pet.

Jessica had begun her search for Gizmo at the animal shelter, where she saw a flyer advertising the services of Missing Pet Partnership (MPP). She hurried home and called its founder, Kat Albrecht. The distraught Jessica needed a professional guide.

Her heart lightened after talking to Albrecht, previously a police officer, who now applies detective skills to search for lost pets. MPP also provides education about lost pets for shelters and rescue groups, so heartbroken owners like Jessica can conduct an informed search before calling a professional search team.

Albrecht encouraged Jessica. "Gizmo is a great candidate for filming a search." Still, doubts of finding Gizmo intermittently daunted Jessica's hopes.

With her well-trained Weimaraner, Rachel, Albrecht visited the home of Jessica's parents, where Gizmo had been living, and an interview began.

"To obtain a standard profile and establish probabilities for Gizmo's loss," said

Albrecht, "I asked about Gizmo's temperament, habits, health, and circumstances surrounding the disappearance."

While answering questions, Jessica wept. "Gizmo has one blind eye," she reported, "but never goes beyond the yard. And, oh," Jessica added to the mix of information, "Gizmo loves to play with his toys in the bathtub."

Albrecht also learned that the absent kitty had no medical problems. And the day before Gizmo had vanished, Jessica's father had seen a strange orange cat in the yard. Mr. Bradshaw had wondered, *Did the big cat challenge him so fiercely that Gizmo fled?*

Categories of probability help define what happened to a pet gone astray. Gizmo was disqualified as a victim of theft, partly because she was not inclined to approach strangers and partly because a domestic shorthair is less in demand than an expensive breed. "The all-white, half-blind kitty, though priceless to his owners," Albrecht explained, "would not appear valuable to a cat burglar."

Wildlife kill, another category, did not apply to Gizmo's circumstances, either.

Injury or the likelihood that the pet was trapped were other possible causal factors. An even less pleasant consideration for the owner is that a missing pet may have been poisoned, struck by a car, or suddenly become ill.

Gizmo scored highest in "territorial displacement." He was lost.

So Albrecht proceeded with an aggressive physical search. She said, "Characteristically, a disoriented cat will hide in silence, ignoring its owner who is calling its name or even passing by while clanging a can of cat food.

"A cat that gets loose from the house will first find the nearest place of concealment and stay there until reaching a threshold of thirst and hunger around the seventh to tenth day. The longer the pet remains secluded, the more scent it deposits and the more comfortable it becomes."

Albrecht prepared to obtain a scent trail by leading Rachel on an investigation of Gizmo's front yard. She collected a scent from Gizmo's toy and presented it to Rachel. "If Rachel picks up a track and

> ### Kitty Wit:
> Few things impede traction better than a fresh waxed floor under the feet of a running cat.

follows that trail," said Albrecht, "I use her tracking talents to follow the path the cat took. If not, I use her as a detection dog and direct her to places I suspect the pet could be hiding or hurt. I might point under a house, a deck, or a stack of rubbish, and give the command, 'Check this!' After sniffing, if Rachel detects the scent, she wiggles her tail, or paws the suspicious spot."

Jessica watched as Albrecht began the routine, glad she had called MPP. Albrecht harnessed Rachel and said, "Take scent, search." But the eager dog picked up no scent in the front yard.

With permission from the next-door neighbor, Albrecht led Rachel through his well-groomed yard. But Rachel showed only mild interest in a shed situated beside the fence.

After guiding Rachel to the next house, they opened the gate upon a giant junkyard with plenty of hiding places for a cat. Albrecht knows her tack. "I directed Rachel's skilled nose through tread-worn tires, a pile of trash, and even a bathtub."

"Suddenly," said Albrecht, "I felt the tension on Rachel's leash. I tightened my hold, intent on leading her on, but Rachel had planted herself. Nothing but Rachel's tail moved on her statuesque body. Frozen in place, with ears up, nose pointed, body stiffened, and short tail wiggling, Rachel fixed her eyes on the cavity of the bathtub.

"I glanced inside the tub," said Albrecht, "and hunched over, puffed up, and hissing was a very frightened, white cat. I grabbed Rachel's collar, backed her up, and called, "He's here, Jessica, I think it's Gizmo!"

Albrecht took Rachel aside. The cat looked terrified with a seventy-five-pound dog eyeing her.

Jessica rushed over. "Gizmo!" Tears coursed down her cheeks. She reached for her cat and hugged and kissed him, while Albrecht looked on with the satisfaction known only to a pet detective.

What were the odds of finding a lost cat who loved his indoor tub in one that was outdoors? A white tub at that? Gizmo had camouflaged well and may have evaded nonprofessionals. The outcome of the search for Gizmo proved the fact that a guided search is more likely to succeed than random exploration. Can those who turn to God expect any less as they search for answers to life's big questions? He who knows all things promises to direct the steps of those who seek Him.

The Tail End:

Abraham Lincoln became a cat lover as a boy in Kentucky. During the Civil War, when Lincoln visited General Grant's headquarters, he heard mewing that led him to three nearly frozen kittens. He rescued them and eventually brought them back to the White House.

Missing Pet Partnership is a national, nonprofit organization dedicated to reuniting lost companion animals with their owners/guardians. MPP offers behavior-based lost pet recovery tips, referrals to lost pet services, and Missing Animal Response (MAR) seminars that train professional and volunteer pet detectives to conduct CSI-like investigative searches. Albrecht is the author of *The Lost Pet Chronicles: Adventures of a K-9 Cop Turned Pet Detective*. Visit her at www.missingpetpartnership.org.

Just Keep Crying

Listen to my cry for help,

my King and my God, for to you I pray.

—Psalm 5:2 NIV

PURR-rayer:

Dear God, make me willing to disclose my needs and appeal for help when I'm stuck. Amen.

Gus was under the weather—literally. The black and white cat lay buried in a snow pile for 16 days, though he never stopped crying for help.

The plump cat was a favorite among Rich and Diane Napierkowski's family of seven. Stubby Gus, nicknamed for his short and thick tail, had grown wide as well as long, an advantage for his survival.

Just days before the Michigan blizzard of 1999, Rich and Diane, with their twin daughters and one of their sons, drove to Florida for a convention and left their cats in the care of a responsible teenage son and daughter. Before leaving, the three children selected snapshots of Gus and packed them in their suitcases to tape on mirrors in their hotel rooms.

Several days after the blizzard, one of the teens called Rich and Diane to report on the snowstorm and on an even worse bit of news. "Mom, Gus hasn't come home since the blizzard hit."

"We were troubled the rest of the trip," said Diane. "The kids called to Gus and searched in the cornfield across the street and around our lake, about 120 feet from the house."

After Rich, Diane and the children returned from Florida, they joined the quest, trekking over 12 acres of property for their beloved cat. Distressed, the family kept questioning. Did someone offer Gus a shelter from the storm? Is he injured? Lost or hurt?

But on a still day, Diane paused at the mailbox to arrange a handful of envelopes in a tidy stack of graduated sizes. "It was then that I heard a soft little meow," she said. "My heart began racing. It sounded like Gus, though I never suspected he was beneath my feet. When I didn't see him, I called to my ten-year-old. David joined me, on high alert, very intent and serious."

Once again, Gus cried.

David brightened. "I hear it, too, Mom!"

"But we didn't realize how close Gus was. David ran down a little road to the lake, listening as he went, and then returned. The meowing faded each time we distanced ourselves from the mailbox. I checked underneath our cars, but each time we got near the mailbox, we heard Gus the loudest. Suddenly, we both shouted, 'It's coming from the snow!'

"David quickly got a shovel, and I ran to the house to get a blanket. It was exciting and also scary," said Diane. "Gus had been missing over two weeks. We hardly knew what to expect or if we'd hurt him as we dug aimlessly.

"Soon, David broke through into a hole the size of a basketball, and we saw Gus' little eyes blink as they adjusted to the sudden and long-awaited light. We were ecstatic! Gus lay in a circular hole he had spun as he tried to break free. David helped him as he wobbled out on weak, stiff legs. His tail tip was chewed and one ear had frostbite. David wrapped

> ### Kitty Wit:
> Cats are smug enough to ignore us when all i
> well and wise enough to wail when all is wron

him in the blanket and we dashed to the house."

By then, his love-necklace had wrapped around a front leg. Gus gobbled the food Diane set before him, until she stopped him, momentarily, to remove the necklace. But Gus hesitated before eating again. For 16 days in his snowy chamber, the necklace had been his only connection to the family. "We put the string of beads back around him, and he returned to his food, seemingly eased," said Diane.

"Shouts of glee, and the news about Gus, passed quickly by telephone to family members not at home. The twins, especially, were incredulous. We canceled all plans for the day so they could rejoice in the return of their cherished friend.

"But that night, Gus awakened the twins with pitiful shrieks. His cries for help must have become a habit," said Diane. "It broke my heart to think he'd cried for days, hearing our calls, yet was forsaken repeatedly."

"Gus was timid by nature," Diane explained. "He liked to hide in the flower patch by the road." Diane suspects Gus had fled to the bed of dry and tangled flowers by the mailbox, when he heard the roaring snowplow which shaped the berm that covered him.

While entombed, he must have licked melted snow that thawed from the warmth of his body. His icy enclosure smelled strongly of urine. And the lifeless flowers that poked through the surface of the snow may have provided airways to his cave.

A couple days after Gus' rescue, he revisited the scene. He sniffed the wet hole, as though recollecting. The rest of the winter, he stayed close at home. On the first day of snowfall the following winter, he refused to go out.

Gus slowly regained the weight he'd lost and also changed in another way.

"He used to be a loner," said Diane, "but not any more. He cries loudly if he has needs."

When Diane home-schooled her children, she expounded the many lessons the family learned from Gus—this one among others. When you need help, just keep crying.

 The Tail End:

Survival depends on the loud cry of helplessness. Cry out and cry on! God hears.

Rich and Diane met while working in an all-you-can-eat restaurant. Now they enjoy eating with their five children ages nineteen to twenty-eight. Family-oriented folks, they opted for home births, homeschooling, and a home business they started twenty years ago. Diane applied several of the "Gus Principles" when she returned to college and earned a degree in biomedical sciences.

Tweety

Then you will know the truth, and the truth will set you free.

—John 8:32 NIV

PURR-rayer:

Dear God, don't let me forsake my convictions when others doubt my word.

In 1947, Sylvester the cat and Tweety the bird costarred in the cartoon film *Tweetie Pie*. Tweety's famous line, "I tawt I taw a putty tat," reminds Hilda "Snooks" Cunningham of the story about her cat and the birds on her property. However, in Hilda's case, she "tawt" she *heard* some "putty tats."

Hilda's husband, Bill, doubted his wife's constant report of hearing cats outside her kitchen window. "Snooks, you're just hearing the birds chirp," Bill would counter. A chorus of birdsong was common on the Cunningham land. Bird feeders mounted on a variety of tall trees attracted yellow finches and other species.

A week earlier Bill and Hilda had driven from their home in Mount Sterling, Ohio, to Johnstown, the home of Bill's brother, where fire had leveled Fred's barn. After pulling his fishing boat from the blazing barn, Fred had telephoned Bill, his favorite handyman. "Why don't you take the boat to your place and restore it for me?"

Bill had agreed. The sixteen-foot runabout collected several inches of rainwater while it sat those first few days on the Cunningham property. During that time Hilda described the sound she heard as the high-pitched mewing of newborn kittens.

Though Bill disputed his wife's notion, he finally inspected the acreage opposite the kitchen window. He also emptied the runabout of rusty fishing gear and returned to tell Hilda, "Snooks, I even checked the boat. You must be hearing the birds tweeting."

But Hilda insisted. "I still say I hear kittens."

Exchanges of this sort continued, until the day Hilda's stepfather, Emerson, came to help Bill with the boat work. While draining rainwater from the hull, Emerson "tawt he *taw* some putty tats!"

"Hey, Bill!" he called. "There's cats in here. Six of 'em."

Bill took a look. "Well, I'll be! Snooks kept saying she heard kittens!" The litter of wet cats, huddled in the belly of the boat, had been sustained with rainwater during the fourteen days since Bill had hauled it from Fred's.

Eager to tell Hilda, Bill and Emerson hurried to the house where Bill readily confessed. "You're right, Snooks! Wasn't birds. We found half a dozen kittens in that boat."

"What a relief!" She sighed. Though surprised at the cats' specific whereabouts, Hilda felt vindicated.

Immediately, Bill telephoned his brother. "Hey, Fred! You got a mother cat, minus her young?"

After Bill explained his question, Fred replied, "I'd figured her kittens suffocated or burned in the barn fire, but I've still got the mother!"

Right away, Bill and Emerson drove the hundred miles back to Fred's to reunite the mother cat with her nearly starved young. The lactating queen welcomed her offspring with plentiful licks.

Yet a sequel to the story still waited. The next day Bill and Emerson resumed the boat project, and again, Emerson "tawt he taw a putty tat." Emerson

Kitty Wit:
After a spat, housemate cats
just hiss and make up.

reached for the overlooked kitten, still alive in the boat, as Bill watched in amazement while shaking his head.

When Hilda heard the news about another "putty tat," she and Bill made a quick decision about the tiny gray tiger. "He's a keeper," said Hilda. "We'll name him Tweety."

Thereafter, Emerson teased Bill any time the topic of birds or cats slipped into a conversation. "What kind of a man can't tell the difference between a cheeping bird and a meowing cat?" Emerson would playfully chide, and Bill would smile.

"My mother was petrified of cats," said Hilda, "so I didn't grow up with them and didn't know how to care for one. But I'd heard about feeding kittens with a doll's baby bottle. I mixed milk and cream with two parts water and fed Tweety every hour."

Long after, Hilda learned that the extra-rich mix could have killed the kitten. Even the vet said, "It was TLC alone that saved that little bugger."

Bill took over Tweety's care when Hilda went back to work the following Monday. After Hilda shared the story with her colleagues, a coworker gave her a starter supply of kitty litter and a soft toy chick. "A small stuffed animal will lessen the kitten's feeling of isolation," she said.

In a blanket-lined Easter basket, Tweety snuggled with the yellow chick and bonded instantly. Chicken is still Tweety's security pet, though its body is now color-faded and missing feet and beak. But if anyone touches Chicken, Tweety hides it for several days.

Interestingly, Tweety favored Bill over Hilda during the sixteen years they shared life together. If not in the basket, Tweety napped in Bill's shoe or on his lap. When Bill passed away, Hilda put his winter jacket on the bed for Tweety. "He slept in the sleeve for weeks," she said.

Many benefited because Hilda held to the fact that she heard kittens. First, she herself was justified; the mewing was, indeed, "putty tats." And Bill benefited; he gained Tweety, a lifetime pet. Also, six kittens found their mother, and Mother-cat found her litter. And not to forget Emerson, who had years of fun jeering Bill about his lack of discrimination. Even Hilda's mother benefited. Her fear of cats lessened through visits with Tweety.

Never forget: everyone profits from the truth.

 The Tail End:

A group of kittens is called a "kindle." A "dam" is the mother of kittens, and a group of older cats is named a "clowder."

Snooks is the secretary-treasurer for the Thoroughbred Horsemen's Health Fund, a division of the Ohio Horsemen's Benevolent and Protective Association ohio-hbpa.com, in Ohio. Hilda said Bill would be proud that Tweety's story was published in a book.

Bibliography

Listed alphabetically by story title

"The Advent of Marshmallow," The Tail End: *The Christian Imagination*, edited by Leland Ryken, Waterbrook Press, 2002, excerpt from Luci Shaw, p. 84.

"Cat Hater Recants," Kitty Wit: quote by Marty Becker from his column "The Bond," *The Spokesman-Review*, Spokane, Washington, August 31, 1999.

"The Cosmopolitan Cat," The Tail End: from the Web site Fact Monster: Science, http://www.factmonster.com/science.html/.

"The Dangers of Paws-sessions," Kitty Wit: permission from North Shore Veterinary Clinic to use posted humor, http://www.whipworm.net/library/LibHumorCat.shtml.

"The Divine Drama," The Tail End: quote from *Desiderata for Cat Lovers: A Guide to Life & Happiness*, Willow Creek Press, 2006, from "Desiderata" by Max Ehrmann, 1927.

"Encounters with Mystery," The Tail End: www.thecatsite.com/Snips/106/Cat-Coat-Colors/html.

"Ex-*purr*-t Guidance," The Tail End: *The Quintessential Cat* by Roberta Altman, Macmillan, 1994, p. 153.

"Foolhardy or Faithful?" The Tail End: quote by Emily Dickinson, http://www.quoteworld.org/authors/emily_elizabeth_dickinson.

"Home Sweet Treetops," The Tail End: quote by Arthur Christopher Bacon; source unknown.

"Hooray for the Birds," The Tail End: list of cat breeds from the Web site Fact Monster: Science. http://www.factmonster.com/science.html/.

"The Indictment of Indifference," words of Christ; Matthew 5:37 NIV; The Tail End: statistics from *The Press-Enterprise*, a California newspaper owned by Belo Interactive, www.PE.com.

"A Litter Bit Goes a Long Way," The Tail End: quote by Charles Dudley Warner, source unknown.

"Mews-eum Security," based on Internet research and AP article, "Felines' venerable role at museum dates to 1764," *The Spokesman-Review*, Spokane, Washington, August 22, 2004; The Tail End: from http://en.wikipedia.org/wiki/Cats_in_ancient_Egypt.

"A Midnight Message," The Tail End: Ray Henry, "Cat sensed when patients will die," Associated Press, 2007. Scripture reference in body of story from John 14:1 NIV; Kitty Wit: source unknown.

"No Kiddin'," The Tail End: *Days to Remember, A Keepsake Book*, written and illustrated by Donna Green, Smithmark Publishers, 1995, pages unnumbered; quote by Marjorie Holmes from page dated December 14.

"No Trick, All Treat," The Tail End: *Cats in the Garden 2002 Calendar*, Fulcrum Publishing, 2002, February and August.

"Only Out of View," Kitty Wit: *Morris* by Mary Daniels, Dell Publishing, 1974, quote, "Robert Redford of catdom," from *New York Daily News*.

"Opportunity Ajar," Kitty Wit: source unknown.

"Particular Person Meets Purr-ticular Cat," The Tail End: http://www.pawsonline.info/feline_statistics.htm.

"Stealing Hearts at the Lighthouse," The Tail End: www.pawonline.info under "familiar cat phrases"; Kitty Wit: permission from North Shore Veterinary Clinic Web site to use posted humor, http://www.whipworm.net/library/LibHumorCat.shtml.

"Stormy Aftermath, Sunny Outlook," quotation from Rosemary, "Picking Up the Pieces," October 24, 2005, and "She's Staying…For Now," October 26, 2005, stories by Virginia de Leon in *The Spokesman-Review*, Spokane, Washington.

"Surviving and Thriving Post 9-11," information and quotes from *San Francisco Chronicle* (10/20/01) and permission granted for use of material posted at the website of the Suffolk County (NY) SPCA. Please note: New York State law requires there to be but one SPCA per county in the State of New York. The Suffolk County SPCA is in no way affiliated with, is not a subdivision of, nor receives any money from the ASPCA, which is a Manhattan-based SPCA. The Tail End: quote from www.thinkexist.com.

"Taxi Cab Chauffeur," The Tail End: tips taken from the article "Traveling with Cats" by Sally Smith at www.thecatsite.com.

"Tongue in Cheek," news brief from *The Spokesman-Review*, Spokane, Washington, January 9, 1997; The Tail End: *Peter's Quotations: Ideas for Our Time* by Laurence J. Peter, Bantam Books, 1977, p. 19; Kitty Wit: quote from www.useful-information.info/quotations/cat_quotations.

"Tweety," The Tail End: *The Quintessential Cat* by Roberta Altman, Macmillan, 1994, p.239.

"When Felon Meets Feline," statistics posted by Tyler Cowen on June 14, 2004 at 02:15 a.m. in online Data Source on www.maugauelrevolution.com; information about Lorton Correctional Complex taken from an article by Peter Pae, *Washington Post*, June 1999; The Tail End: *You and Your Cat* by David Taylor, Knopf, 1995, p. 35; Kitty Wit: permission from North Shore Veterinary Clinic Web site to use posted humor, http://www.whipworm.net/library/LibHumorCat.shtml.

"The Wonder of Winnie," The Tail End: *You and Your Cat: A Complete Guide to the Health, Care and Behavior of Cats* by David Taylor, Knopf, 1995, pp. 32–33.

"You Rang?" Kitty Wit: quote from George Burns in "Why We Love Cats," by Anne Fadiman, *Life* magazine, October 1994, p. 80.